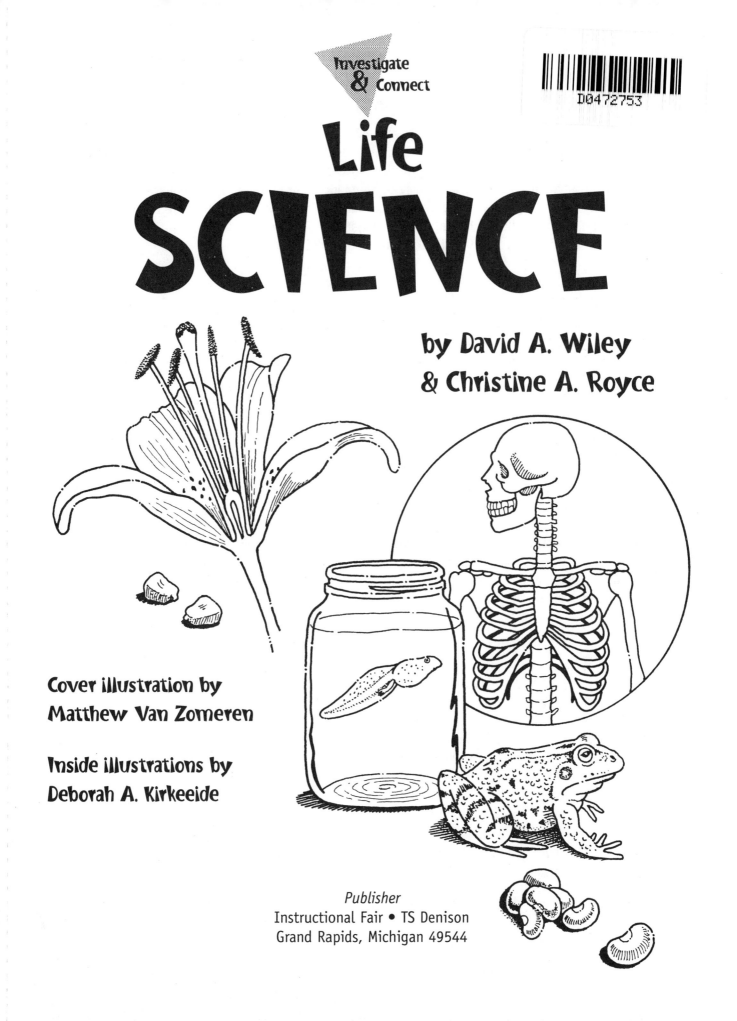

Investigate
&
Connect

Life
SCIENCE

by David A. Wiley
& Christine A. Royce

Cover illustration by
Matthew Van Zomeren

Inside illustrations by
Deborah A. Kirkeeide

Publisher
Instructional Fair • TS Denison
Grand Rapids, Michigan 49544

Instructional Fair • TS Denison

About the Authors

David A. Wiley, Ed.D. is Chair and Associate Professor at the University of Scranton in Pennsylvania. He has over twenty-five years in education and is a frequent presenter of classroom teaching strategies to elementary and middle school teachers. Many of his publications and presentations center on the theme of teaching across the curriculum using science and children's literature. A triple hitter, Dr. Wiley holds his Bachelors, Masters, and Doctorate from the Science Education Program at Temple University. His main research interests include the integration of science instruction across the school curriculum by using the S-T-S theme, and the use of children's literature to enhance the teaching of science in the elementary and middle grades.

Christine A. Royce is currently the Academic Dean at Bishop Hannan High School in Scranton, Pennsylvania. She has nine years teaching experience at the elementary through high school level. Presently a doctoral student in Science Education at Temple University, she holds her Bachelors in Elementary Education and Masters in Curriculum/Instruction and Administration and Supervision. She sits on the CBC-NSTA Outstanding Science Trade Book Review Panel and serves as a manuscript reviewer for *Science and Children* (NSTA publication). She was named the 1997 Presidential Awardee for Excellence in Mathematics and Science Teaching for Pennsylvania.

Credits

Authors: David A. Wiley & Christine A. Royce
Cover Illustration: Matthew Van Zomeren
Inside Illustrations: Deborah A. Kirkeeide
Project Director: Debra Olson Pressnall
Editors: Debra Olson Pressnall & Karen Seberg
Cover Art Production: Matthew Van Zomeren
Graphic Layout: Deborah Hanson McNiff

Standard Book Number: 1-56822-477-X
Life Science
Copyright © 1999 by Ideal • Instructional Fair Publishing Group
a division of Tribune Education
2400 Turner Avenue NW
Grand Rapids, Michigan 49544

Table of Contents

How to Use This Book

As classroom teachers we are well aware of the *myriad tasks* that face you on a daily basis in your professional life. Time is your worst enemy. Research, planning, and preparation are all activities which must precede instruction. This book was written in an attempt to assist you in preparing, in a time-efficient way, for quality science instruction. The structure of this book was designed with you in mind. The book is divided into a number of sections. The first section deals with how the book can be used in an inquiry-based environment. Information is also provided on how trade books can be selected for your classroom as well as a number of web sites that you and your students can use to find additional information.

Subsequent sections of the book are referred to as modules and provide you with the in-depth information, activities, and connections to help you in your classroom. Features of every module include:

- **Science background:** Provides a brief explanation of the science concepts needed for a basic understanding of the science discipline being discussed. A number of diagrams are included to assist in clarification of the ideas presented. More importantly, references to the activities are also provided in context within the section.

- **Annotated bibliography:** This comprehensive list of books includes a brief summary of each title. This bibliography was written to assist you in locating children's literature that can be used with each activity.

- **Activities:** Each activity is presented in a lesson plan format that provides you with information relating to the objectives that the activity addresses, a list of materials needed for the activity, and the procedure to follow in conducting the activity. A section on related children's literature specific to the activity is given and the books listed are described in the annotated bibliography. The final section of each activity consists of connections to other subject areas that may be explored. Inquiry-based student lab pages are provided for most of the activities to assist you in the lessons.

As you use this book it is important to realize that activities can be adapted to meet the needs of your students and your classroom environment. There is no set formula for accomplishing this task. The expert on your students' capabilities and behavior is you. We cannot make absolute suggestions as to how you will adapt anything in this book to your particular situation with your particular students. Each of the activities can be adapted for students who are very talented simply by letting them do more of the exploring. You may wish to ask more questions at the end of each investigation, or have students use journals to record predictions, prior knowledge, and then what they learned from the investigation. You may ask them how their results can be applied in the real world around them. These strategies are effective in making the activities more challenging for the students.

Each of the activities can be adapted for students who are not skilled in science investigation simply by giving more direction. Depending on the activity, you may prefer to lead the students through the activity by example, step by step, with the entire class in unison. For some students it may be best to read and review the instructions as a group before beginning the investigation. Perhaps the best procedure for some activities is to have the students complete one task each day over a period of several days. Some of the activities within this book may not be appropriate for your students to complete. In that case, you may want the students to simply watch, and/or take notes, and/or answer questions regarding activities you choose to do as demonstrations.

For the activities that you choose to do as student-centered, hands-on and minds-on science experiences, you have many choices for organizing your class. You may consider grouping the students in your classroom; in most activities, groups of two to five can be effective. While large groups require fewer materials and equipment as a class unit, they are sometimes difficult to manage. Large groups may also cut down on the active participation of each student. Groups of three are favored by the authors, although the research on ideal group size is not definitive. The key is to structure the activities in a way that works for you as the manager of a classroom environment.

The materials, including equipment and supplies, required for each activity are appropriate for a small group or individual. Many of the listed items are inexpensive or easy to locate; while some science equipment must be purchased if not available in your school. For sources of the equipment, you may wish to consider commercial suppliers if you have a budget for purchasing materials. If you only have a small budget for science, you may consider contacting your senior high school science department as a source of materials and equipment, such a balances. In most science departments, supplies of the kind required in this book are not rare. For example, hydrochloric acid is usually stored in concentrated forms in gallon jugs, and making a dilute solution for you does not represent a problem for the science specialist. In fact, being used as a resource by an elementary/middle school teacher would be a compliment for most high school science teachers.

Inquiry-Based Instruction

Individual Differences

Most teachers realize after their initial contact with teaching that not all students and not all classes are going to be able to learn at the same levels as other students or other classes. This is especially true with teaching science to elementary/middle school students. In the elementary school classroom, great differences in both ability and background experiences exist between classes and even among individual students in each class. Taking these conditions into account is an important aspect of planning for effective instruction in science. The differences can range from the specific kinds of experiences each student has while very young to the social structure in which the student is raised. The degree of familiarity with the natural environment, for example, may be different in the eyes of an urban student than the view of a Native American. Some students may be familiar with the sensations like "losing your stomach" while flying in airplanes, while others may only have a passing familiarity with the same sensation as experienced on a Ferris wheel ride. Accounting for these differences makes this aspect of planning especially important with the approach favored by the authors, the inquiry approach. An examination of the students, their abilities and their backgrounds, can save a great amount of time and frustration on the part of both student and instructor.

What Is Inquiry?

The inquiry approach to science teaching involves more than simply asking students questions about science content. Inquiry includes three components as follows: Students must identify questions and problems that precede answers in the learning process, process information mentally to achieve meaningful understanding, and students must be actively involved in the learning (Cairn, 1993). The term *inquiry*, as used in this book, reflects the three components of inquiry as identified above, and the activities within this book utilize all three components. The objectives for activities represent the questions (problems, topics, or issues) to be studied. The instructional sequences given within the activities is presented with the assumption that students can perform the activities and be, thus, active learners. Further, questions are offered to guide the students toward an understanding of the science that will be both meaningful and persistent.

Levels of Inquiry

What makes a lesson an inquiry lesson, and is all inquiry the same? To answer this question, it is important to understand that there are three segments in any lesson involving an investigation. In the first segment, a problem (or topic or issue) must be identified for investigation. In the second, an appropriate methodology must be established for the accomplishment of the objectives of the lesson. Finally in the third, the conclusions must be drawn as a result of the investigation. The process of inquiry can be adjusted to meet the needs of any group of students by providing more or less information in each of these segments, and by expecting the students to answer correspondingly less or more. At least three levels of inquiry exist and make this form of teaching very different from expository teaching. The various levels of inquiry, from expository (none to very little inquiry) to full inquiry (with the teacher giving little or no information) are summarized below:

EXPOSITORY TEACHING

In expository teaching, the teacher establishes all aspects of the inquiry lesson by establishing what problem will be taught, how the problem will be approached, and the teacher will even draw conclusions for the class. This method is, in some circles, known as the "talking head" and is, unfortunately, a dominant form of instruction in science education. "The present science textbooks and methods of instruction, far from helping, often actually impede progress toward scientific literacy. They emphasize the learning of answers more than the exploration of questions, memory at the expense of critical thought, bits and pieces of information instead of understandings in context, recitation over argument, reading in lieu of doing" (American Association for the Advancement of Science, 1990, p. xvi). Too often, a book becomes the single focus of all learning in science. One study states that "90 percent of all science teachers use a textbook 95 percent of the time" (Bonnstetter, Penick, & Yager, 1983, p. 3). Thus the text becomes the single source of information and the single source of activity for over 95 percent of the time. While expository teaching is an efficient technique to communicate large amounts of information, it is certainly not inquiry.

PRIMARY LEVEL OF INQUIRY

An initial experience with inquiry can be found in the experience of virtually all teachers. At the primary level of inquiry teaching, the teacher establishes the problem and the methodology, but allows the students to draw their own conclusions. This is the format for the majority of lab investigations to which many teachers are exposed in their own education. Usually given by a lab handout, the objectives (problem) of the investigation are established. The handout also provides the methodology through a carefully sequenced series of steps, and then leads the students with questions to draw their own conclusions. Since the teacher usually has already directly taught the concepts involved in the lab exercise, this requires very little inquiry since the student already knows the answer. Only when students are given the freedom to draw their own conclusions does inquiry begin. When the students ask themselves "What does this mean?" they will, perhaps, begin to build their own frameworks for understanding within the common experience of the structured investigation.

SECONDARY LEVEL OF INQUIRY

The secondary level of inquiry represents a higher level of inquiry in that the students are asked to establish their own methodologies to yield their own conclusions to a problem that is posed by the teacher. In the elementary classroom, and even at higher levels, the selection of methodology is most often monitored through a requirement of a "proposal" of some sort. In this way, the teacher can actively guide the student toward a methodology that will not lead the student down a path that goes nowhere. The teacher can consider the capabilities of the students and the limitations of equipment available to the students. If the teacher permits the students to pursue an investigation for a long period of time and the students do not see success, then the students can be easily frustrated. The teacher becomes less of a fount of knowledge and more of a guide for student experiences. It is this involvement of the teacher that gives the primary and secondary levels of inquiry the name "guided inquiry."

FULL INQUIRY

In the elementary school, it is very rare to see open inquiry. In open or third level inquiry, the students select the topic to be studied, the methods to be used, and then draw their own conclusions that result from the investigation. This type of inquiry can be independent investigations, such as those in "junior academy of science" projects and in some "gifted student" programs, but is rarely used in the mainstream of elementary education. The reason is, simply, that most of the students at the elementary level are not ready or do not possess the cognitive development to deal effectively with all three aspects demanded by open inquiry. Due to their lack of experiences, it is unreasonable to expect that most elementary students are able to select a problem for investigation that is appropriate to a science concept being studied. Guided inquiry, the preferred methodology at the elementary level, avoids the complexities involved in open inquiry while providing a shared experience in which the learning of science can be enjoyed with a minimum of frustration.

Planning the Investigations

The lessons included within this book are written at the level of primary inquiry. That is, they have expressed objectives, and a carefully sequenced series of steps that permit a successful guided-inquiry investigation. However, the science lessons suggested here can be altered to be suitable for any group of students by adapting the lessons appropriately. To make the investigation less an inquiry and more an expository type of approach, give the students more information regarding the results. Perhaps inclusion of a "You should see . . . which is . . ." statement would accomplish just that. If you wish to increase the amount of inquiry involved in the lessons, then avoid giving step-by-step directions and allow the students to construct their own procedures. (See reproducible form on page 8.) Again, the use of the "proposal" is encouraged for this type of investigation. Use your professional judgment to decide whether to increase or decrease the level of inquiry expected of groups of students.

LAB

Planning Your Investigation

Questions: _____
(Purpose) _____

Materials _____
Needed: _____
_____
_____

Procedure: Design an experiment.

Steps in Your Procedure

1.

2.

3.

4.

5.

Results: Record observations and/or collect data. (Examples: Keep a log. Draw diagrams. Make a chart or table.)

Conclusion: _____
_____
_____

Choosing and Using Trade Books

National Use of This Methodology

The use of children's literature in the teaching of science has become an increasingly popular methodology that has garnered much national attention. Many elementary teachers are using literature in their science programs as part of a literacy-based instruction because it blends reading, writing, and talking in a learning environment. Teachers realize that there are many possibilities for developing activities from these books that allow students to explore science in a hands-on/minds-on environment. Further, we know that science-oriented trade books are very popular with children. Children's trade books can serve as a valuable reading resource. A year-long study done by a librarian in New York shows that science books are the second most popular books among children (Mechling & Oliver, 1983, p. 37). For purposes of this methodology, trade books or children's literature can be defined as any "commercially available publication that can be used as a supplement to your classroom text" (Kralina, 1993, p. 33). This may include fiction as well as nonfiction books.

However popular this practice is, this methodology is not without naysayers. While some research supports the use of children's literature, other studies suggest that there can be problems with using children's literature in the teaching and learning of science. It is questionable which side has more supporting evidence. It is quite obvious in the world of practice that many teachers put a great deal of time into the integration of trade books into an activity-based science curriculum. However, in a literature search on the topic, very little quantitative support for the use of trade books to teach science was found. One quasi-experimental study showed that by combining the instructional time allotted for reading and science, students' achievement in science was at significantly higher levels (Romance & Vitale, 1992). However, another study suggests that "children's literature may not be an effective science resource" due to its ability to foster misconceptions (Mayer, 1995). It is clear that this methodology is being utilized by elementary teachers throughout our schools since many of the articles in journals are based on classroom experiences—a kind of research in action rather than quantitative research. Qualitative research confirms the value of the following suggestions: Given the degree to which this methodology is embraced, it is important for classroom teachers to understand both the benefits and pitfalls of using children's literature for science instruction.

Benefits to Reading

One of the primary benefits in using trade books is the possibility of addressing interest areas and reading levels of students. Researchers (Tunnell & Jacobs, 1989; Holmes & Ammon, 1985; Simon, 1982) have shown that the use of trade books increases the students' interest levels, improves reading skills, and allows for individuality and variability for students with different reading abilities. This methodology has also shown to be an important tool in aiding students to develop an appreciation of reading for pleasure (Simon, 1982). When children read for pleasure, science trade books offer the opportunity of teaching the students when students do not realize that they are learning. (Simon, 1982).

Not only does the use of trade books address the varying reading levels of students, there is also the possibility to increase reading abilities. Research [Cohen, 1968; Cullinan, Jaggar & Strickland, 1974; Eldredge & Butterfield, 1986 (cited in Tunnell & Jacobs, 1989)] goes on to show that the use of children's literature in the reading program had a statistically significant outcome in terms of increased reading levels compared to the traditional approaches to reading instruction. Gee & Olson (1992) also point out that the use of trade books in a primary science curriculum strengthens students' basic skills and helps them read more difficult books.

Children in the elementary grades are taught how to read using stories. When they attempt to read science textbooks they find that reading this material is very different from what they are accustomed to in reading class. Textbooks offer a heavy concentration of factual information that is expressed in an expository format rather than the narrative format found in reading. Therefore, by using children's literature, students are being presented factual and conceptual information in the manner that parallels their reading instruction, allowing for both science and reading to be strengthened.

Benefits to Science

When children's literature is carefully chosen, many benefits can occur. These benefits include addressing the individual needs of learners through a variety of materials; allowing them to explore science and the scientific method in a different perspective; providing students with knowledge from a wholistic perspective about their natural world; encouraging them to develop critical thinking abilities through reading; and enlarging their vocabularies (Janke & Norton, 1983).

One of the benefits that exists is the availability of science trade books for use within the elementary/middle school classroom. In recent years, an abundance of elementary trade books that teach science have made it possible to teach nearly every science unit with this methodology (Crook & Lehman, 1990). By having a greater selection of trade books from which to choose, teachers can easily meet the individual needs of children by providing several selections on the same topic rather than attempting to use one textbook.

When a familiar format is used instead of a textbook, each student is not as overwhelmed with the facts and has an opportunity to view science from a different perspective. Through the use of children's literature, students are able to see science as an integral part of their daily lives (Stiffler, 1992). Children are also able to make connections to real life applications when facts are presented versus when they are taught only through traditional means. Once students see science as a part of their lives, attitudes toward science improve as does their attitudes toward scientists.

The use of trade books also allows the teacher to use children's interests to guide the teaching of science (Simon, 1982). Crook & Lehman argue that "if they are engaged in the content of the book, drawn to its detailed illustrations, photographs, paintings, woodcuts, diagrams, children read and learn with enthusiasm" (1990, p. 22).

The question of science achievement within this methodology has been addressed in studies by Romance & Vitale (1992); Dole & Johnson, (1981); Anderson, (1993). These studies show that the incorporation of children's literature into a science program increased the students' science knowledge level, as positive attitudes toward science. Norris' (1989) study showed no significant results but did state that "although enthusiasm for literature was not measured . . . students enjoyed listening to the variety of stories. They would come in each day eager to hear another story. Their enthusiasm for books was very obvious." Additional, non-quantitative studies by Butzow & Butzow (1988); Butzow & Butzow (1990), and Pond & Hoch (1992) show that there is a strong but undefined interrelationship between reading and science when children's literature is used. Research has shown that students may be able to better understand science information when it is presented in a trade book. The trade book contains a story line which is easier to follow than attempting to comprehend facts presented in a science textbook.

The use of trade books in science also aids in the explanation of abstract science principles that are often presented in a confusing way in textbooks. The story line in a trade book is easier for students to follow than the facts that are presented in a textbook (Butzow & Butzow, 1989). The means to help students overcome misconceptions also exists when trade books are used to convey information (Miller, 1996). By using children's trade books to explain abstract concepts and counter misconceptions, students are also developing critical thinking skills (Kralina, 1993). Due to this reading modification, it is argued that using trade books can introduce the student to the scientific method, transmit knowledge about the world, and permit an opportunity to experience the excitement of discovery (Janke & Norton, 1983). Additionally, there is a natural connection between science and reading. It has been shown that many of the skills developed for problem-solving in science are the same skills used by children in reading (Carter & Simpson, 1978). Thus, the research supports the practice of teaching science through children's literature.

Suggestions for Choosing Children's Literature

Although children's literature provides many benefits, one must be careful to select literature of high quality. The following guidelines offer points to consider when selecting and using literature.

APPROPRIATE THEME CONTENT

The first suggestion for selecting literature is to choose trade books that are clearly related to a subject matter theme (Pond & Hoch, 1992; Mayer, 1995; Janke & Norton, 1983). Many forms of assistance to the classroom teacher are available, including the annual list of the National Science Teachers Association—Children's Book Council "Outstanding Trade Books in Science" list which is published in March of each year. There are also a number of articles in journals that present collections of trade books organized into appropriate themes. Such articles typically list appropriate resources for a single or multiple themes and are often followed by a listing of the cited trade books organized by grade level.

GRAPHIC ORGANIZERS

A second suggestion is to use graphic organizers to clarify the science content of the trade books. With many science concepts comes a measure of mystery. Utilizing graphic organizers adds the important aspect of visualization and often makes the concept more concrete and less mysterious in the minds of children (Schwab & Coble, 1985).

OPPORTUNITY TO INVESTIGATE

The third suggestion is to include with the scientific information, opportunities for students to experiment with the concepts. Barrow, Kristo, & Andrew (1984) explain that hands-on/minds-on activities are needed since "according to Piaget's theory, teaching that uses only reading or telling for science is inappropriate for children at the preoperational and concrete operational stages" (p. 188).

Cautions for Use

As noted earlier, not all the literature on the use of trade books is supportive of this methodology. Some of the recent literature has introduced a note of caution in the enormously popular move to teach science using trade books. One of the reasons for such caution is that the accuracy of scientific content sometimes suffers in a trade book's attempt to represent otherwise complicated information. Misinformation is not the only form of inaccuracy that makes its way into children's trade books. Errors of omission or an attempt to simplify the information presented may also be misleading to students.

Some additional warnings regarding the use of science trade books include insuring that stereotypes are avoided, that illustrations are accurate and labeled, that texts encourage scientific ways of thinking, and that science content is clarified by the organization of the book (Janke & Norton, 1983).

Checklist for Selecting Literature

The following checklist can be used in evaluating children's trade books for use in teaching science.

Content

Does the book have:
• an appropriate reading level?
• the interest range for your students?
• an appropriate amount of detail?

Does the book address:
• the subject matter?
• the intended concepts and facts to support them?

Does the book:
• avoid stereotypes?
• encourage analytical thinking?

Can the book:
• be connected to the curriculum's scope and sequence?
• be connected to the textbook?
• be connected to other subject areas?

Illustrations, Pictures, and Diagrams

Do the illustrations, pictures, and diagrams:
• show accurate material?
• have labels that explain them?
• reflect the material that is presented in the text?
• complement the book's text?

Accuracy and Authenticity

Does the book:
• present information in an accurate way?
• present misconceptions or partial truths?
• contain current science information?

Portals for Learning: Web Sites

PLANTS

http://versicolores.ca/SeedsOfLife/ehome.html
> This is a bilingual (English and French) celebration of the seed. It includes information about fruits and seeds, information on seeds and mankind, and links to more site relating to seeds.

http://www2.garden.org/nga/EDU/Home.html
> The National Gardening Association offers a homepage for students. It highlights its newsletter called *Growing Ideas* which provides activities for the classroom.

http://questions.burpee.com/burpee/
> This page is the Burpee Seed homepage where students can ask questions and receive answers for their questions. Some of the students' questions are then posted on the homepage.

http://www.plantamnesty.org/
> This is the homepage of an organization dedicated to the proper use of plants in architecture. It is an excellent resource for information and speakers on this topic. Also displays humorous pictures of "bizarre yard-art architecture."

http://www.weather.com/gardening/
> The Weather Channel's homepage has a section on gardening that provides information on daily precipitation forecasts, soil treatments, and monthly planting maps for specific crops.

http://www.hcs.ohio-state.edu/hcs/TMI/TR2/pmTOC.html
> This homepage contains a searchable database of 1,444 images and descriptions of horticultural materials. The images can be located by name, category, feature, and by pests.

http://aggie-horticulture.tamu.edu/kinder/sgardens2.html
> The site offers activities and on-line games that cover the topics of soil, air, and water.

INVERTEBRATES

http://www.public.iastate.edu/~jlmc/escan/WdInverts.html
> This site is offered by the Environment Sciences Communication Activities News by Iowa State University and defines the kinds of invertebrates found in the woodland.

http://www.public.iastate.edu/~jlmc/escan/WaterInverts.html
> This site is offered by the Environment Sciences Communication Activities News by Iowa State University and defines the kinds of invertebrates found in the waterways.

http://www.aqualink.com/marine/reef.html
> This commercial site offers a number of excellent articles with valuable information regarding coral and the coral reef.

http://www.public.iastate.edu/~jlmc/escan/PrInverts.html
> This site is offered by the Environment Sciences Communication Activities News by Iowa State University and defines the kinds of invertebrates found in the prairie.

http://www.cfe.cornell.edu/compost/invertebrates.html
>   Offered by Cornell's science and engineering program, this site offers information and diagrams of the organisms involved with composting.

http://research.amnh.org/invertebrates/
>   This American Museum of Natural History site lists research and research staff involved in a variety of projects dealing with invertebrates.

http://204.186.19.24/museum/invertpics/Invertebrates
>   Many simple labeled drawings of many common invertebrates can be viewed at this web site.

http://imc2.lisd.k12.mi.us/msc1/invert/key.html
>   This site offers an easy-to-understand and usable dichotomous key for the identification of common invertebrates.

http://www.umesci.maine.edu/ams/inverts.htm
>   This site contains a listing of www sites regarding invertebrates organized by phyla and by source.

http://www.butterflywebsite.com
>   This site offers facts, descriptions, and pictures of butterflies and moths.

VERTEBRATES

http://netvet.wustl.edu/pix.htm
>   An electronic zoo that provides web links to a variety of pictures and information about animals.

http://www.chebucto.ns.ca/Environment/NHR/index.html
>   This site is peppered with images to compliment its listing of the world of birds and butterflies. Additional content is under construction.

http://www.nature.ca/english/gameherp.htm
>   An on-line quiz about reptiles and amphibians that provides a picture of fourteen different reptiles and amphibians and asks the viewer to classify them. Then submit your answers and see how well you did.

http://sparky.cs.nyu.edu:19234/welco.htm
>   This web site is the entry point to the Casiano Zoo and provides web links to areas for mammals, birds, reptiles, fish, amphibians, and invertebrates.

http://pubs.usgs.gov/gip/dinosaurs/
>   This site, maintained by the United States Geologic Survey, includes information and links to other sites regarding the most-used elementary science topic.

http://nyelabs.kcts.org/nyeverse/shows/s311.html
>   A web site related to "Bill Nye the Science Guy" and his "Sites of Science." This particular page discusses marine mammals, provides detailed information about different types of marine mammals, and includes video clips.

http://www.sfzoo.com/html/map.html
>   The home page for the San Francisco Zoo

http://santaanazoo.org/
>   The home page for the Santa Ana Zoo

http://www.sandiegozoo.org/
    The home page for the San Diego Zoo

http://www.neaq.org/
    The home page for the New England Aquarium

THE HUMAN BODY

http://www1.sympatico.ca/healthyway/TOC/toc_1.html
    This Canadian site offers an indexed listing of links that includes sites with information related to the parts of the body and health issues.

http://www.innerbody.com/htm/body.html
    The educational site provides information on ten systems of the human body with simplified graphics for students.

http://www.deacons.cambs.sch.uk/internet/curric/science/sci3f.html
    The web site provides information about the human body, including pictures, sounds if applicable such as in the beating heart and information.

http://odp.od.nih.gov/
    This is the official site for the Office of Disease Prevention at the National Institutes of Health. Offers other links to sites.

http://www.sd68.nanaimo.bc.ca/schools/coal/grade4/gr4life.html
    This web site is created by a fourth grade teacher and offers activities related to the human body, senses, and body systems.

http://ificinfo.health.org/brochure/10kid2.htm
    A site designed for children to help them choose healthful snacks and foods. It also gives suggestions on staying healthy through physical activity.

References

Anderson, L. S. (1993). "The Effect of Literature-based and Written Composition-based Instructional Strategies on Children's Understanding of Herpetology" (Doctoral dissertation, University of South Carolina, 1993). *Dissertation Abstracts International,* 54: 1230A.

Barrow, L. H., & Salesi, R. A. (1982). "Integrating Science Activities through Literature Webs," *School Science and Mathematics* 82: 65-70.

Barrow, L. H., & Kristo, J. V., & Andrew, B. (1984). "Building Bridges between Science and Reading," *The Reading Teacher* 38 (2): 188-192.

Bonnstetter, R. J., Penick, J. E., & Yager, R. E. (1983). *Teachers in Exemplary Programs: How Do They Compare?* Washington, D.C.: National Science Teachers Association.

Butzow, C. M., & Butzow, J.W. (1988). *Science, Technology, and Society as Experienced through Children's Literature.* (ERIC Document Reproduction Service No. ED 294 141).

_____ (1989). *Science through Children's Literature: An Integrated Approach.* Englewood, CO: Teacher Ideas Press.

_____ (1990). "Science through Children's Literature: An Integrated Approach," *Science Activities* 27 (3): 29-38.

Caduto, M. J., & Bruhac, J. (1994). "There's Science in That Story!" *Instructor* 103 (7): 42-44, 48, 92.

Cairn, A. A. (1993). *Teaching Science through Discovery* (7th ed). Columbus, OH: Merrill.

Carter, & Simpson (1978). "Science and Reading: A Basic Duo," Science Teacher 45 (3): 20.

Crook, P. R., & Lehman, B. A. (1990). "On Track with Trade Books," *Science and Children:* 22-23.

Dole, J. A., & Johnson, V. R. (1981). "Beyond the Textbook: Science Literature for Young People," *Journal of Reading* 24: 579-581.

Galda, L., & MacGregor, P. (1992). "Nature's Wonders: Books for a Science Curriculum," *The Reading Teacher* 46: 236-245.

Gee, T. C., & Olson, M. W. (1992). "Let's Talk Trade Books," *Science and Children* 29 (6): 13-15.

Holmes, B. C., & Ammon, R. I. (1985). "Teaching Content with Trade Books: A Strategy," *Childhood Education* 61: 366-370.

Janke, D., & Norton, D. (1983). "Science Trades in the Classroom: Good Tools for Teachers," *Science and Children* 20 (6): 46-48.

Kralina, L. (1993). "Tricks of the Trade," *The Science Teacher* 60 (9): 33-37.

Mayer, D. A. (1995). "How Can We Best Use Children's Literature in Teaching Science Concepts?" *Science and Children* 32 (6): 16-19, 43-44.

McDonald, J., & Czerniak, C. (1994). "Developing Interdisciplinary Units: Strategies and Examples," *School Science and Mathematics* 94 (1): 5-10.

Mechling, K. R., & Oliver, D. L. (1983). *Science Teachers' Basic Skills.* Volume 1. Washington, D.C.: National Science Teachers Association.

Miller, K. W., Steiner, S. F., & Larson, C.D. (1996). "Strategies for Science Learning," *Science and Children* 33 (6): 24-27, 61.

Norris, L. K. (1989). "The Effects of Integrating Children's Literature into the Kindergarten Science Curriculum. (ERIC Document Reproduction No. ED 314 712).

Orlich, D. C. (1989). "Science Inquiry in the Commonplace," *Science and Children* 26 (6): 22-24.

Pond, M., & Hoch, L. (1992). "Linking Children's Literature and Science Activities," *Ohio Reading Teacher* 25 (2): 13-15.

Romance, N. R., & Vitale, M. R. (1992). "A Curriculum Strategy That Expands Time for In-depth Elementary Science Instruction by Using Science-based Reading Strategies: Effects of a Year-long Study in Grade Four," *Journal of Research in Science Teaching* 29: 545-554.

Schwab, P. N., & Coble, C. R. (1985). "Reading, Thinking, and Semantic Webbing," *The Science Teacher* 52 (5): 68-71.

Shaw, D. G., & Dybdahl, C. S. (1992). "Rain Forests: Do They Hold Up the Sky?" *Preventing School Failure* 37 (1): 19-25.

Simon, S. (1982). Using Science Trade Books in the Classroom," *Science and Children* 19 (6): 5-6.

Stiffler, L. A. (1992). "A Solution in the Shelves," *Science and Children* 29 (6): 17, 46.

Tunnell, M. O., & Jacobs, J. S. (1989). "Using "Real" Books: Research Findings on Literature-based Reading Instruction," *The Reading Teacher* 42: 470-477.

PLANTS

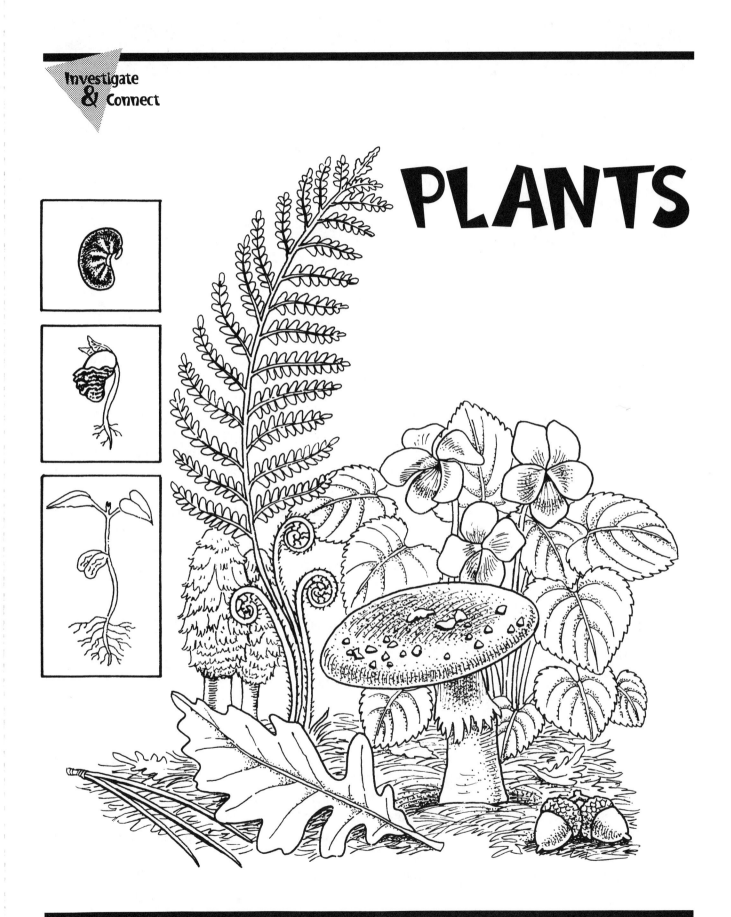

The Plant Cell

See Portal for Exploration "Who Grows What?"

Plants are living things and are the basis of life on this planet. Their study is an important part of science and is called botany. Plants can be defined by the following characteristics: they have the potential to or actually do grow; they transform energy which includes metabolism and, in some plants, photosynthesis; they form new individuals in reproduction; they react to environmental pressures such as heat and light; and they have an organic composition or are carbon based. Scientists disagree as to exactly what it is that causes plants to be alive or, in general, what specific definition could be used for life. However, the characteristics given can be used for an operational definition for the condition we call living.

As in all living things, the cell is the basis of life. While we generally think of plant cells as very small units, cells of some plants can attain lengths of 50 cm or longer. Yet there is a generalized cell structure that is common to virtually all plant life. This structure sees a cell as a mass of living material called *cytoplasm,* in which a variety of organelles are located. Each of the organelles has a specialized function that it accomplishes to make the cell a living system. However, the mass of cytoplasm and the organelles it holds would simply fall apart if not held in place by the *cell membrane.* The membrane is a continuous envelope in which the cell's structure is held. The semipermeable membrane allows materials such as water to pass through it while holding the cytoplasm and its contents in place. In plants, unlike animal cells, the cell membrane is surrounded by a more rigid structure called the *cell wall.* The purpose of the cell wall is simply to provide rigidity to the plant structure. Although not all plants have the stem and root system that one associates with the word "plant," all plants seem to have this basic structure.

See Portal for Exploration "Building an Animal Cell," Invertebrates Module

The organelles that are most common in the plant cell include the nucleus, the endoplasmic reticulum, mitochondrion, ribosomes, chloroplasts, and vacuoles. The nucleus is the control center of the cell. It contains the genetic material that imprints the cell with its structure and its function. It is the *nucleus* that initiates the processes of cell division which enables the cell to replicate. The *endoplasmic reticulum* is a very long flattened system of membranes that fold back and forth on each other in a somewhat curious pattern; this maximizes surface area yet provides a circulation system within the cell. *Mitochondrion* are often oval-shaped structures seen rarely with light microscopes. They serve as the powerhouses of the cell. The chemical reactions that occur within these small and complex organelles provide the energy on which the cell lives. The *ribosome* is a very small structure, also rarely visible in light microscopes. Its function includes protein synthesis. It is within this structure that new material is produced that permits cell growth, maintenance, and division. Several ribosomes are found floating freely in cytoplasm, on the surface of the endoplasmic reticulum, and sometimes within an organelle called the *chloroplast.* The chloroplasts, organelles specific to green plants, contain the chemical, chlorophyll, that permits a green plant to produce its own sugar. The *vacuole* is a space within a plant that holds cell sap, a mixture of materials produced by the cell. The vacuole can often be seen as a large light-colored space within the cell. The size of the vacuole increases with age and its shape varies with the internal pressure of the cell. Interestingly, the pigments of many of the autumn colors of leaves are colors contained in cell sap of vacuoles. The colors deepen as a result of a combination of genetic responses to environmental factors such as light and temperature.

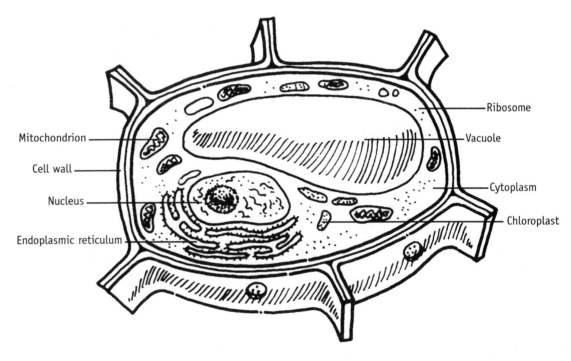

Parts of a Plant Cell

See Portal for Exploration "Moving through a Membrane"

Much of the life processes of a plant depends on a process called *diffusion*. Materials in nature tend to move from areas of high concentration to areas of low concentration. This is evident in a situation when the aroma of a simmering onion can be detected from a room far from the kitchen in which it is cooking. In much the same way, salt added to the bottom of a glass of water will eventually make the entire contents of the glass taste salty as the concentration of salt and water equalize throughout the glass. In cells, movement of needed materials occurs in a similar manner as the circulation of the cytoplasm carries and distributes those materials throughout the cell. The cell membrane does play a significant role in the movement of materials into and out of the cell. While water can move through this membrane, salt cannot. Water passes through the cell membrane moving from the area of high concentration of water to where the concentration of water is lower. If a normal cell is dropped into a container wherein the salt concentration is higher than the salt concentration within the cell, the cell will see a movement of water toward the lower concentration of water. As the water moves out of the cell in an attempt to equalize the concentrations, the cell will shrink due to the loss of water. If the water outside a cell is less salty than the concentration of salt inside of the cell, the water movement will again be toward the area of a lower water concentration in an effort to equalize the situation. The water outside the cell will move inward through the semipermeable membrane and cause a swelling of the cell. This process of osmosis is important in maintaining appropriate water concentrations and pressures within the plant cell.

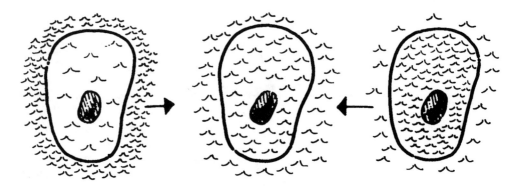

The Diffusion Process

Vascular Plants

Plants do occur in two major groups—those with supporting and conducting tissues (stems and vascular bundles) and those without these tissues. Those plants without these structures include algae, fungi, lichens, liverworts, and mosses. Plants with supporting tissues can be broken down into two subgroups—those producing seeds and those that do not produce seeds. Plants that do not produce seeds are the ferns and club mosses.

SEED-PRODUCING VASCULAR PLANTS

Those plants that produce seeds include the conifers that usually produce seeds in cones and the flowering plants that range from the fragile orchid to the giant sequoia. Some of these flowering plants produce a seed with a single seed leaf (monocotyledon), such as the grass seed and corn, and some produce a seed with two seed leaves (dicotyledons), such as a pea or bean. The germination of these seeds are different in important ways, but all will produce flowers.

See Portal for Exploration "Where Are Your Roots?"

For the purposes of discussion, a generalized plant will be used to emphasize the structures and functions of a plant's principal parts: root, stem, leaf, flower, and seed. Anchoring the plant to the ground is a root system that reaches under the soil. The roots grow and advance through the soil, using internal pressures to create spaces that permit expansion of the root into the space. This force can be significant, breaking rock into pieces, which stimulates the formation of soil or as seen when a tree planted too close can lift sidewalks out of place. The root system of a plant also serves a second function, the absorption of water and minerals from the soil. This water and mineral mixture supplies critical micro-nutrients and water necessary for the life process to occur within the plant. Roots are of generally two types. One type of root has a very thick and strong central root growing nearly straight down from the plant. This *taproot system* is different than the *fibrous root system* in which a network of roots branch out from several main roots and spread over a large area. Some plants have *specialized root systems,* such as the aerial roots hanging from black mangrove, the knees of cypress, or the prop roots of the corn plant.

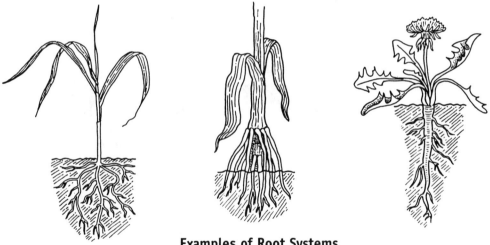

Examples of Root Systems

See Portal for Exploration "What Is the Function of Stems in Plants?"

The stem of a plant connects the root system to the other parts of a plant, including the leaves. The stem gives structural strength to the plant as it raises up toward the sunlight in an unexplainable phenomenon known as phototropic. There are two very important groups of tubes within the stem. Some groups of tubes (vascular bundles) conduct raw materials to the leaves from the roots, and another group distributes the life-giving sugars, produced in the leaves, throughout the plant. Xylem, also known as the "wood" of a plant, conducts the raw materials upward, and phloem is the distribution system for the finished products. The growth of woody plants over time creates new layers of xylem each year, resulting in the appearance of annual rings in cross sections.

*See Portal for
Exploration
"Looking at Leaves"*

*See Portal for
Exploration
"What Color Light
Helps Plant Growth?"*

The leaf is the food production center of the plant. Its structure could be considered a part of the stem, but while the stem grows for the entire length of the lifetime of the plant, the leaves function for only one or several seasons before falling away. The conducting vascular system of the leaf can be seen as the vein system. The venation can be *parallel,* with the system of veins running nearly parallel between typically long leaves. Venation can also be *pinnate,* with one main vein and smaller veins extending from this main vein along its entire length. Finally, venation can be *palmate,* with several main veins extending radially from the point of leaf blade attachment to the petiole or the stem of the leaf. Some leaf structures contain only one blade connected to one petiole, but others have many blades connected to a long petiole that branches to each side. Single blade leaves are called *simple,* and many blade leaves are called *compound* leaves. The type of leaf and its venation are often used in the process of plant identification. Regardless of the type of leaf, its primary purpose is the production of food for the plant. While the leaf is exposed to sunlight, the chlorophyll captures the sunlight and converts it to usable energy to drive the process known as photosynthesis. Without leaves, the process of photosynthesis would not occur in this generalized plant.

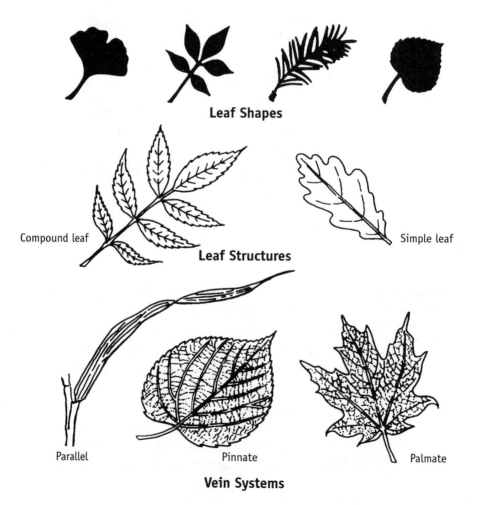

Leaf Shapes

Compound leaf

Simple leaf

Leaf Structures

Parallel

Pinnate

Palmate

Vein Systems

The flower is the reproductive organ of our generalized plant. Its purpose is to produce seeds. Structurally, a flower consists of the petals, sepals, stamen, and the pistil that leads to the ovary. The *petals* are the most noticeable portion of the flower. They are typically the colorful display that provides the aesthetic beauty of the organism. They provide the blue of violets and the red of roses. *Sepals* are petal-like structures that are usually smaller than the petals but can, on some plants such as clematis, be as large or larger than the petals. They are usually arrayed around the outside of the petals but are absent in some types of flowers. The sepals and petals surround the stamen and pistil. *Stamen* are long, thin structures from which pollen is released. The *pistil* is the part of the flower that can catch pollen and conduct it to the *ovary*. *Pollen* has the ability to fertilize an egg in the flower's ovary to produce a seed. Some flowers can pollinate themselves (such as wheat and peaches), and others need to be cross-pollinated between individual plants (carrot and avocado). Insects play an important role in the pollination process as they physically rub against stamen and pistils during their searches for nectar. An insect such as a honeybee can pick up pollen on its body and deposit the pollen on the pistil of the same flower or on other flowers as it continues its journey. Pollination is important, for it is the pregnant ovary of a flower that becomes a fruit as well as the bearer of seeds to produce a future generation.

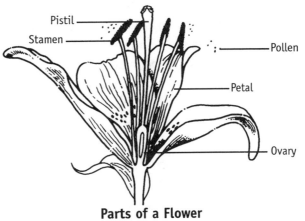

Parts of a Flower

See Portal for Exploration "How Does Your Garden Grow?" and "What Does Your Garden Need to Grow?"

The seed is a very familiar topic to most people who understand that corn and sunflower seeds can provide important nutrient value to us as human beings. Rarely, however, do we dissect these structures to find that each seed is really a nursery for an embryo of the plant from which the seed was taken. Although a seed does not grow until a stimulus causes its germination, the seed has the potential to grow, and therefore, is termed a living thing. The outside of a seed consists of the *seed coat,* a heavy covering that protects the interior parts of the seed. Some seed coats are so strong that they need to be scorched by fire before they can germinate, or begin the growth process. Inside the seed coat is the *embryonic plant* with a *radicle* that develops into the first root of the plant, and the *hypocotyl* which serves as the embryonic stem that connects the radicle to the *cotyledons,* or seed leaves. The end of the embryo is called the *plumule* and is the point from which growth is the most rapid. This embryo is usually found embedded within the endoplasm, an oil- or starch-rich protein mix that provides the nutrients to feed the germinating plant until the plant begins to take over the feeding processes with the onset of photosynthesis.

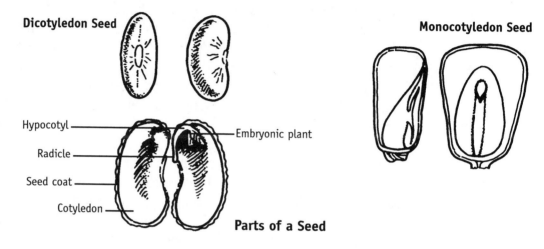

Dicotyledon Seed

Monocotyledon Seed

Hypocotyl

Radicle

Seed coat

Cotyledon

Embryonic plant

Parts of a Seed

See Portal for Exploration "Monocot or Dicot? What Is the Difference?"

In *monocotyledon* (corn) seeds, the seed germinates and the plumule reaches directly skyward in the search for sunlight. In *dicotyledon* (bean) seeds, a loop is formed as the seed germinates and the hypocotyl reaches skyward first. If conditions of light are right, the hypocotyl will continue to grow and draw the cotyledons and plumule out of the ground. The difference in the germination process is one that can be studied easily and within a narrow time frame. Yet it is not totally understood how or why this difference has developed in the history of plant evolution.

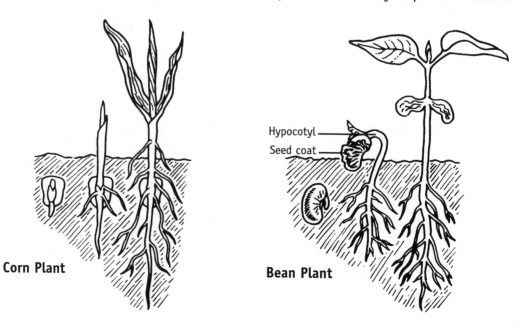

Corn Plant

Hypocotyl

Seed coat

Bean Plant

SEEDLESS VASCULAR PLANTS

Club mosses, each looking very much like princess pine trees, the common horsetail, which looks like single sprigs of a thin fern, and the often ornate ferns, together make up a group of plants that have vascular structures but do not produce

seeds. These plants produce spores instead of seeds. A spore is the very tiny, usually one-celled, mechanism of reproduction for this kind of plant. The individual spores can germinate and form a structure that has stamen- and pistil-like parts which, in turn, have the capacity to produce another plant. This group of plants is among the oldest living vascular plants on earth, and geologists have discovered many more of these plants which lived as early as the middle of Devonian Period (about 390 million years ago). Many of the early ferns were not like the ferns of today, but were seed ferns and could grow to tremendous heights. Yet, the size of today's ferns, often thought of as the beautiful small plants of highway embankments or forest glens, can actually reach a height of 18.3 m (60 feet) in the form of the fern trees of the tropics. These ferns can have leaves 3.66 m (12 feet) long!

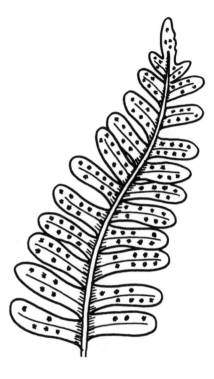

The club mosses are interesting plants that can grow in soil or in the crevasses of fallen tree bark. The plants usually range from 1.2 to 1.5 m (2 to 5 feet) in height, taking on the appearance of tiny princess pine trees. Small structures at

the ends of the "branches" look like cones and are the source of the spores that keep the species alive. The plant was, fortunately, very successful over time with the fossil history of club mosses directly associated with the giant trees of the Devonian Period reaching heights of 30.5 m (100 feet) or more. Today, the club mosses are common in both the tropics and subtropics, but are, unfortunately, too "cute." They are often needlessly hunted and sold as Christmas decorations.

Horsetails are plants usually found in wetland areas or other wet environments such as ponds. They are anchored by an underground system of root-like structures that give rise to aerial branches. The stems are marked by leaf scars giving the plants a noticeable system of ridges. The leaves and the branches, if present, occur as tightly twisted structures. At the ends of the leaves, they take on a bushy appearance which likely explains their common name of horsetail. Although this plant now ranges to about a meter in height, outside of a few tropical varieties which may be 10 times taller, the ancient horsetail of the Carboniferous Period grew commonly to 12.2 meters (40 feet).

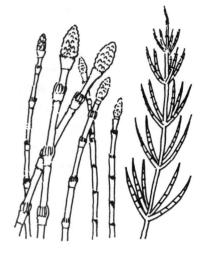

It is the growth of these kinds of plants in the swampy regions of the world that gave rise to today's coal fields. As the ancient ferns and horsetails of the Carboniferous grew, died, and piled up as debris on the floor of huge ancient swamps, they were covered with still more debris before they were decomposed. In the oxygen poor water of the coal swamps, decomposers were rare, and the debris continued to pile up until geologic events caught up with them. Sediment covered the material sealing it from any further decomposition. Uplifting, the resulting pressure and heat of being buried by sediment, and additional heat and pressure associated with metamorphism, formed bituminous (soft) coal. If continued heat and increased pressure were applied, anthracite (hard) coal was formed. A significant amount of the power we enjoy in today's world owes thanks to these ancient forms of life that lived and died in the swamps of the Carboniferous Period, more than 300 million years ago.

Non-vascular Plants

The non-vascular plants are sometimes called the low plants, due to their structural simplicity, and include the algae, fungi, lichens, liverworts, and mosses. Algae include single-celled varieties and other larger varieties of simple plants that usually contain chlorophyll, but never develop the characteristics we associate with plants such as stems, roots, and leaves. Most are marine and include the pond scums, the seaweeds, and phytoplankton. Phytoplankton are single-celled varieties of algae that live in the top 30 meters (98 feet) or so of the oceans. Some oceanographers claim that up to 90% of the world's basic fuel (captured sunlight that is fixed by photosynthesis into a usable form) can be attributed to phytoplankton. One particular algae found in ponds has an interesting pattern of chloroplasts. When viewed under a microscope, the pattern can be observed as a set of spiral markings along the entire length of each cell—thus the name of this particular blue-green algae, spirogyra. Another type of algae found in cold Pacific Ocean waters is the giant kelp which is known to reach lengths of 31 meters (100 feet). While most algae are marine, some are terrestrial. Terrestrial algae can be found in or on soil, growing on snow, and even on animals or in mines deep in the earth. In most cases, the green "moss" that grows on the northern side of tree trunks is actually an algae. This simple plant is usually photosynthetic, but some varieties are not. The dinoflagellate, a single-celled algae, is a member of the yellow-green algae that feeds more like an animal on nutrients in the water to which the flagellum drives it. A population explosion of dinoflagellates in nutrient-laden water can stain the water and gives rise to the phenomenon of the red tide. Poisonous to humans, the dinoflagellates are potentially harmful if shellfish that fed on them are then consumed by humans.

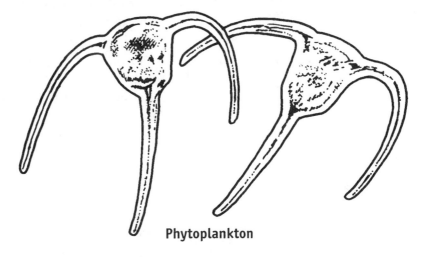

Phytoplankton

Algae, while photosynthetic during the day, use oxygen in their life processes at night. A sudden bloom of algae in a pond or stream can potentially "choke" the water of the pond or stream, driving its dissolved oxygen levels to near zero. Many desirable forms of life can be displaced by the conditions that result from the hearty and fast-growing algae. It is, then, a potential contributor to the degradation of water supplies. Yet, algae is a very old form of life on earth that may have provided the food and oxygen responsible for the rise of most other forms of life. Today, the evidence for this is found in some algae that produce carbonate compounds stored within their cells. This makes the algae resistant to the ravages of time and preserves some algae as "humps." Some similar "humps" can be found in rocks older than 600 million years and are, it is thought, evidence of algal life in the earliest of the geologic eras, the Precambrian. It may not be accidental that green algae predates virtually all other evidence of life. It is the algae that now provides the base of the global food web, and it was also probably true in the distant geologic time.

*See Portal for
Exploration
"Growing Mold"*

*See Portal for
Exploration
"Name That Plant"*

Fungi are non-green plants which lack chlorophyll and have a structure characterized by a network of filaments called hyphae. These hyphae provide the functions required to obtain nutrients from the environments in which they are found. Fungi are plentiful in soil and in and on dead plant and animal remains. Fungi can be seen as mold on many organic materials and may arise as quickly as overnight. Writings found in ancient texts cite the dangers of a variety of fungi, including rusts, mildews, and blights. Many fungi are known by farmers as threats to crops, driving up prices of food by driving down the supply. Leaves roll up, fruits grow in deformed shapes, blossoms drop off, and entire plants can be dwarfed by these diseases. Foresters know fungi that attack trees. One particular fungus is the chestnut blight which will bring an end to the commercially desirable native chestnut tree. The elm is also threatened by Dutch elm disease, accidentally introduced to the United States in 1930s. In humans, fungi cause such minor infections as ringworm and athlete's foot as well as the more serious valley fever. While much more rare, valley fever is a systemic infection of fungi that grow parasitically, similar to yeast cells. It usually causes mild reactions but can, on rare occasions, be fatal. On the other hand, some gill fungi are edible as mushrooms. Careful identification is required to insure that the mushrooms being eaten are not poisonous. The only truly safe mushrooms to eat are those purchased from a reputable vegetable dealer.

Non-vascular Plants

Liverworts and mosses are very similar in appearance. Typically growing in masses on rocks, rotting wood, or the bark of trees, these plants are anchored to soil or other surfaces by small structures that act much like root hairs. These structures absorb moisture and minerals for the plants. Liverworts and mosses reproduce from spores that develop from sex organs borne on the top surface of the plants. Some liverworts, called leafy liverworts, grow as masses with leaves growing to both sides and sometimes down from the axis. The mosses can be recognized because of the symmetry. Their leaves grow from all sides of a central axis. In many mosses, the leaves arise from vertical stem-like structures and, in others, the leaves spring upward on branches. A common type of moss, sphagnales, form the common bog, or peat, mosses. Their commercial value is easily recognized.

Lichens are not single plants but each consists of two plants, an alga and a fungus, working together. This relationship is one in which each partner provides essential functions to the plant unit. The alga provides the energy-yielding food and vitamins. The fungus provides the plant with water and mineral material. Without one or the other contributor, the plant could not survive. This relationship is called mutualism. Lichens are important in the formation of soil, for as the small structures extending into the cracks and crevices of the rock grow and expand, the rock is broken down through this mechanical process. Lichens, then, are often the first plants that grow on the surface of bare rock, and they are responsible for triggering soil formation.

Soil

*Portal for Exploration
"Is Your Soil Best or
Mine?"*

The importance of soil to plants should be a very obvious topic. Not only is it the surface on which terrestrial plants grow, but soil is the provider and supporter of plants. Its composition, the size and chemical make-up of its components, as well as its thickness, in part determines what can grow in it. For aquatic plants, many of the same concerns apply, although the state of matter is different. Measurements are made to soils to find the relationship of humus, sand, silt, and clay. Humus is made from the remains of plants and animals that lived in the soil. Clay is a type of mineral material that is very fine grained and becomes sticky when wet. Silt is also a fine soil mineral material, but it does not become sticky when wet. It is typically the "mud" carried by streams. Sand is made from pieces of broken rock in grain sizes that are larger than silt or clay. It is the relationship of these components that provide the pore spaces which may fill with life-giving water. The movement of water through the soil is a very important characteristic, when considering how many water soluble minerals may be carried away in a moist climate. Soil chemistry has great significance in determining the acidity of the soil. A rule of thumb is that if a region receives more than 25 cm of rain each year, its soil will be acid. In climates such as these, the addition of a pH moderating limestone powder may be necessary to remediate the effect of the acid. On the other hand, some plants (most evergreens, for instance) grow better in acidic soil. For some plants, an annual treatment with a commercial acid compound may be best.

Plants require different amounts of elements to function. The essential elements important to plants include carbon, hydrogen, and oxygen. These materials are easily obtained from the air and from the water held in the soil. It is interesting to note that the carbon that contributes to the formation of sugars in photosynthetic plants comes from the carbon dioxide in the air, not from the soil. The macro-nutrients needed in smaller amounts include nitrogen, phosphorous, sulfur, potassium, calcium, and magnesium. Micro-nutrients needed in very small amounts include iron, copper, manganese, zinc, molybdenum, boron, and chlorine. Fertilizers, both commercial and organic or "green" fertilizers, act to provide supplies of these materials to the soil. Whether in the form of manure scattered by a farm spreader or in a spike placed in a potted plant by a gardener, all fertilizers do the same thing by providing the plants with needed nutrients.

The formation of soil is a very slow process. It may take up to 500 years for 25 cm (1 inch) of topsoil to be formed. Rocks are broken down into smaller pieces, first by lichens and then by other plants. The breakdown of the parent rock continues as dead organic debris begins to add to the mixture of broken rock. Water action adds to the process as some minerals are dissolved, carried away, and contribute to the buildup of soil elsewhere. However, humankind's ability to destroy soil is outstripping nature's ability to build it up. Some natural mechanisms such as glaciers, regularly remove soil from one place to be deposited in another. Societies' actions, building cities on floodplains, disruption of streams and drainage systems, and irresponsible construction techniques, can increase the rate of erosion. Overgrazing and full-tillage farming can result in increased erosion of the soil from the land, moving it to bays and estuaries where its darkening effect can negatively influence the plant growth in those areas. It is estimated that 7% of the world's cropland looses its topsoil each decade. Loss of the world's soil is a situation that must be recognized as a serious problem that has impact on the human condition.

Portals for Learning: Literature

Aliki. *Corn Is Maize: The Gift of the Indians.* Harper Collins, 1976.
This story tells how the Native Americans relied heavily on the corn crops that they grew. The book shows diagrams on corn and its growth.

Arnosky, J. *Crinkleroot's Guide to Knowing the Trees.* Bradbury Press, 1992.
An illustrated guide to trees and woodland plants, the author gives detailed information on how to identify the different species.

Bolwell, L., & Lines, C. *Where Plants Grow.* Wayland Publishers Limited, 1983.
This book examines the different types of plant vegetation that are found throughout the world and describes why each plant best survives in these areas.

Brooks, F. *Protecting Trees and Forests.* Scholastic, 1994.
This Usborne conservation guide offers a great amount of information on trees and forests through colorful pictures and factual information.

Buscaglia, L. *The Fall of Freddie the Leaf.* Charles B. Slack, 1982.
This story, often used for counseling purposes, tells the story of Freddie the leaf, who buds one spring and begins to grow throughout the summer and finally dies in the fall. The story incorporates information about the seasonal changes of a tree.

Butterfield, M. *Flower.* Simon & Schuster, 1991.
For young readers, this book describes how seeds are dispersed and how flowers are pollinated. Once the reader gains an understanding of the two events, it further describes what a seed needs to grow.

Carle, E. *The Tiny Seed.* Picture Book Studio, 1987.
This book describes the story of a flowering plant's life cycle as it progresses through the seasons. The pictures in this book are very colorful collages.

Cole, J. *Plants in Winter.* Thomas Y. Crowell, 1973.
A child discovers what happens to plants in the winter throughout this narrative text. Each question leads to more questions about what is happening to the roots in the winter, the stems, and how plants get nutrients. It ends with the child wanting to become a plant scientist.

dePaola, T. *The Popcorn Book.* Scholastic, 1978.
Although this book is on the topic of popcorn, it provides the reader with a great deal of information about corn, how it is grown, and products made from the plant. A good book to use with ethnobotany.

Dowden, A. O. *From Flower to Fruit.* Thomas Y. Crowell, 1984.
An in-depth book on how flowers mature into seed-bearing fruit. The author uses sketches and pictures of seeds and fruits to accompany the text.

Ehlert, L. *Growing Vegetable Soup*. Scholastic, 1987.
Tells the story of a young child who experiences growing all of the vegetables needed for vegetable soup, from the planting of the seeds through the harvesting of the vegetables.

Ehlert, L. *Planting a Rainbow*. Harcourt Brace Jovanovich, 1988.
This colorful book describes how a mother and child plant a rainbow of flowers in the family garden.

Ehlert, L. *Eating the Alphabet*. Harcourt Brace Jovanovich, 1989.
Introduces the reader to the world of vegetables through the alphabet. Pictures could be used to discuss where plants grow.

Ehlert, L. *Red Leaf, Yellow Leaf*. Harcourt Brace Jovanovich, 1991.
This story is about the growth of an apple tree from a seedling to a mature tree through the eyes of a child. The book could be used to discuss the maturation of trees.

Ford, M. *Sunflower*. Greenwillow, 1995.
A young girl plants a sunflower and watches over it by making sure it has the necessary things to grow. In the end, the sunflower produces seeds which are eaten by birds, insects, and the girl.

French, V. *Oliver's Vegetables*. Orchard Books, 1995.
A young boy who is visiting his grandfather's farm learns to eat different vegetables as he picks them.

Gackenbach, D. *Mighty Tree*. Voyager Books, 1992.
This book tells the story of three different seeds that are planted in a forest. Each seed grows into a pine tree but is found to have different uses within society: one becomes paper and products, the second a Christmas tree, and the third a home for forest creatures.

Gibbons, G. *The Seasons of Arnold's Apple Tree*. Scholastic, 1984.
The reader learns how Arnold uses his apple tree throughout the seasons. The story also describes what physical characteristics of the tree change during each season.

Gibbons, G. *From Seed to Plant*. Holiday House, 1991.
Explains in a very clear format what happens as seeds are planted, when they begin to germinate, and how they grow into plants.

Heller, R. *Plants That Never Ever Bloom*. Scholastic, 1984.
In a narrative format, this factual book explains about non-flowering plants and their method of reproduction and growth.

Heller, R. *The Reason for a Flower*. Scholastic, 1983.
Offering good information, the book explains the purpose of flowers.

Kalman, B. *How a Plant Grows.* Crabtree, 1997.
Through a chapter approach, this book examines the different stages of a seed's development. Beautiful color pictures are added to assist the reader with understanding concepts such as germination, pollination, and growth.

Kroll, S. *The Biggest Pumpkin Ever.* Holiday House, 1984.
Two mice, a country mouse and a village mouse, become interested in the same pumpkin and help it grow through proper feeding and watering all without knowing about the other's efforts.

Krudop, W. L. *Something Is Growing.* Atheneum, 1995.
Peter plants a seed one morning in a small patch of dirt on a city street. As he takes care of it, he and his neighbor watch it grow into a giant plant that overtakes part of the street and city. A good book to show that plants can grow anywhere.

Madenski, M. *In My Mother's Garden.* Little, Brown and Company, 1995.
In this story, a young girl plants some pansies as a birthday present for her mother.

Moore, I. *The Vegetable Thieves.* Viking Press, 1983.
Vegetables are being stolen from a garden planted and cared for by two mice. The mice, who are proud of their garden, attempt to track down the thieves.

Muller, G. *Around the Oak.* Dutton's Children's Books, 1994.
Children observe an oak tree in a forest throughout the year. This is a good book to demonstrate changes in plants during the seasons.

Nelson, J. *How Does My Garden Grow.* Modern Curriculum Press, 1990.
In this story, two girls carefully plant a garden and watch it develop and grow throughout the summer.

Overbeck, C. *How Seeds Travel.* Lerner Publications, 1982.
The factual book provides real pictures on how seeds are dispersed from place to place by the wind, water, and animals. Additional information is given on how seeds function in plant reproduction.

Perrot, A. S. *The Oak.* Creative Editions, 1993.
This book describes the physical characteristics of an oak tree and how it reproduces.

Primavera, E. *Plantpet.* G. P. Putnam's Sons, 1994.
A young boy finds a life-form in his back yard that is fond of gardening but almost loses it by not understanding what his "plantpet" needs.

Relf, P. *The Magic School Bus: Plants Seeds*. Scholastic, 1995.
A tie-in book to the television series, this book discusses a variety of topics about seeds and their growth into plants. Ms. Frizzle takes her class on an adventure that shows students how seeds germinate, plants are pollinated, and insects use nectar.

Rylant, C. *This Year's Garden*. Bradbury Press, 1984.
A great book that tells the story of the seasons as it follows a rural family's garden, it discusses crops growing and being harvested at different times.

Seuss, T. *The Lorax*. Random House, 1971.
This classic describes what happens as natural resources are depleted over time. An entrepreneur moves into an area where trees are very abundant and begins a business that chops down the trees. This book offers an excellent starting point for the discussion of trees as a natural resource.

Siracusa, C. *The Giant Zucchini*. Hyperion Books, 1993.
A mouse and a squirrel grow a giant zucchini for the county fair. However, when they sing to the zucchini, it possesses magical powers. A good book to discuss what a plant needs to grow.

Stevens, J. R. *Carlos and the Squash Plant*. Northland Publishing, 1993.
Written in both English and Spanish on the same page, this folktale tells the story of a young boy who ignores his mother's directions to take a bath. Eventually a plant sprouts in his right ear and he has a difficult time trying to hide it under his hat.

Tresselt, A. *The Gift of the Tree*. Lothrop, Lee and Shepard, 1972.
The story traces the life cycle of a tree. It provides shelter for animals while it is living and also as as it begins to decay.

Weisner, D. *June 29, 1999*. Clarion Books, 1992.
A young girl designs an experiment that launches vegetable seeds into the upper atmosphere. As time goes on, large vegetables begin falling to the ground much to her dismay. An excellent book to use when teaching the process skills.

Wilner, I. *A Garden Alphabet*. Children's Books, 1991.
This easy reader offers a series of rhyming verses that use the letters of the alphabet as a starting point. The rhymes tell the readers how a garden in planted, grows, and the insects and creatures that assist the garden.

Zion, G. *The Plant Sitter*. Harper and Row, 1959.
A young boy agrees to watch a plant for a neighbor and does such a good job of taking care of the plant that it takes over the house.

Who Grows What?

Purpose:
- Describe the value of specific crops to various enthic groups.
- Plant a garden that represents crops grown in your local area.

Materials Needed:
seeds (e.g., corn, wheat, barley, potatoes, sunflowers, pumpkins, beans, and squash)
soil
large planting containers or plot of land

Introduction: One of the goals of science, technology, and society is to have students gain an appreciation and understanding of scientific events that affect society while at the same time drawing conclusions about these events. In this activity students will read *Corn Is Maize: The Gift of the Indians* by Aliki and discuss ethnobotany.

Setup: If possible, select a site on your school grounds to plant a small garden or plan on growing plants indoors in large plastic containers. Follow directions on the packets for planting the seeds.

Procedure:
1. After reading *Corn Is Maize* have the students identify where corn products are used today and in which products we use. Create a poster display of the products using corn as a base by bringing in the packaging from food products.
2. Plant a indoor/outdoor garden with different types of plants that are found in different cultures, such as corn, wheat, barley, potatoes, sunflowers, pumpkins, beans, and squash.

Behind the Scenes: This activity will take quite a while to complete since students will need to plant, maintain, and care for the garden. This might be an activity to last all spring. Have students plant the garden once frost is no longer a concern. Students and families can sign up to extend the activity by taking care of the garden all summer long on a weekly basis. At the beginning of the next school year, celebrate the harvest by having a picnic with the students who cared for the plants. Hopefully, some of the produce can be enjoyed by all.

Literature Links:
Aliki. *Corn Is Maize: The Gift of the Indians.* Harper Collins, 1976.
Ehlert, L. *Growing Vegetable Soup.* Scholastic, 1987.
Rylant, C. *This Year's Garden.* Bradbury Press, 1984.
Stevens, J. R. *Carlos and the Squash Plant.* Northland Publishing, 1993.

Portals for Expansion:
Science • Read Aliki's book (describing pollenization and fertilization) and follow with a book about insects and their necessity in some pollenization of flowers.
Social Studies • Research what crops are the basis of diets throughout civilizations in the world. Compare climate conditions, land terrain, and other features of these areas.
• Host an "International Day" party and ask parents to make traditional ethnic food dishes to share with the students. Allow students to dress up in traditional costumes.
Art • Create murals that tell the story of planting crops in different civilizations.
Language Arts • Ask students to bring in traditional recipes from their ancestors and create a classroom recipe book.
• Write letters to cereal companies and request information on why they use certain types of grains as compared to others.
Health • Conduct a blind taste test or have a taste off with cereals that are mainly rice, wheat, and corn.

Moving through a Membrane

Purpose:
- Describe osmosis by conducting an activity, observing the phenomenon, and writing the results.
- Conclude that a common egg is actually a very large, single cell.

Materials Needed:

2 eggs	3 small bowls
water	salt
vinegar	corn syrup

Introduction: The common chicken egg is actually one cell. The largest single cell is the egg of the ostrich. While expensive, they can be obtained from farms that raise ostriches. The shell of an egg is a protective layer of calcium carbonate that is deposited around the cell membrane. This activity uses the selectivity of the cell membrane to allow water to pass back and forth, but the shell must first be removed. The activity, then, is in two parts. The first part is the process to remove the calcium carbonate by dissolving the shell in vinegar, and the second step shows osmosis, or the passage or diffusion, of a material through a semipermeable membrane (the inner membrane of the chicken egg).

Procedure: See instructions on student lab sheet.

Answer Key For Questions:
1. Cell
2. The egg in sugar water became larger than the other egg. The egg in salt water was smaller.
3. The egg in sugar water absorbed water and changed in size.
4. The egg in salt water shrunk in size because water left the egg.
5. They will shrink and shrivel if left in the water for a long enough period of time.
6. There are salts found in both the pool and the oceans which cause water to move out of the cells in your hand.
7. They would shrink in size because water would leave the cells.
8. Freshwater is important for moving water into cells and replacing existing water that may have salts in it.

Literature Links: Dowden, A. O. *From Flower to Fruit*. Thomas Y. Crowell, 1984.
Kalman, B. *How a Plant Grows*. Crabtree, 1997.
Relf. P. *The Magic School Bus: Plants Seeds*. Scholastic, 1995.
Weisner, D. *June 29, 1999*. Clarion, 1992.

Portals for Expansion:

Social Studies
- Write about countries in which pure drinking water is not as plentiful as it is in the United States and about the processes they use to obtain freshwater.

Mathematics
- Weigh each of the eggs before and after the experiment to calculate the percentage change in the weight of the egg caused by the movement of water.

Moving through a Membrane

Procedure: **Dissolving the Eggshell**
1. Record how a chicken egg feels when holding it. Describe the shell.
2. Carefully place two eggs, without cracks, into a small bowl. Cover them completely with vinegar.
3. Keep the eggs in the vinegar for 24 hours.
4. Rinse the eggs after the shells have been removed in clean water. Describe how the eggs feel and look.

Eggs not Soaked in Vinegar	Eggs Soaked in Vinegar

Observing Osmosis
1. Fill two bowls about two-thirds full with water.
2. Stir 30 mL (2 tablespoons) of salt into one bowl of water.
3. Add 118 mL (½ cup) of corn syrup to the other bowl.
4. Place one rinsed egg in each bowl.
5. Observe what happens to the eggs during the next 12–24 hours. How does each egg look now? Draw each egg to show what has happened.

Sugar water	Salt water

Questions:
1. The egg is surrounded by a membrane without any smaller divisions. What is the term that describes this unit building block of life?
2. Which egg became larger? smaller?
3. Which egg shows that material can move *into* a cell?
4. Which egg shows that material can move *out* of a cell?
5. If you put your hand in salt water, what will happen to the cells of your hand?
6. Why is your hand "shriveled up" after you come out of the ocean or swimming pool?
7. What would happen to the cells in your body if you drank salt water?
8. Why is freshwater important to cells in your body?

Where Are Your Roots?

Purpose:
- Recognize the two major types of root systems (taproot and branching root systems) by growing one of each and noting the differences.
- Recognize common foods as originating from roots.

Materials Needed:
toothpicks
2 tall clear plastic drinking cups or large plastic jars
sweet potato
small carrot
water

Procedure: See instructions on student lab sheet.

Answer Key For Questions:
1. Answers will vary. For example, depending on the outcome of the experiment the sweet potato should produce leaves.
2. Answers will vary.
3. The carrot plant should develop a root system.
4. Carrot
5. Sweet potato
6. We eat the root of the plant.

Literature Links:
Ehlert, L. *Growing Vegetable Soup*. Scholastic, 1987.
Ehlert, L. *Planting a Rainbow*. Harcourt Brace Jovanovich, 1988.
French, V. *Oliver's Vegetables*. Orchard, 1995.
Gibbons, G. *From Seed to Plant*. Holiday House, 1991.
Kalman, B. *How a Plant Grows*. Crabtree, 1997.
Moore, I. *The Vegetable Thieves*. Viking Press, 1983.
Relf, P. *The Magic School Bus: Plants Seeds*. Scholastic, 1995.
Weisner, D. *June 29, 1999*. Clarion, 1992.

Portals for Expansion:

Social Studies
- Interview individuals from other regions or countries to find out if their foods are similar to your foods.

Language Arts
- Write a report about farmers who raise potatoes for sale and profit.

Science
- Try this activity with radishes, beets, or other tubers that are found in the produce section of the grocery store. Use containers of damp sand instead of water to sprout roots.

Mathematics
- Start two identical plants in containers. Compare their growth when one plant is feed a commercial plant food with the water. Measure and graph the height of the plants over the length of the activity.

Where Are Your Roots?

Procedure: **Sweet Potato**

1. Fill a cup about one third of the way with water.

2. Put the pointed end of a sweet potato in the water.

3. Use toothpicks to hold the sweet potato in place.

4. As time passes, keep the level of the water at the same height.

5. Draw a picture of your sweet potato plant every week. Keep the pictures together to make a book that shows its growth.

Carrot

1. Fill a cup about half way with water.

2. Put the pointed end of a carrot in the water.

3. Use toothpicks to hold the end just under the water just like the sweet potato above.

4. As time passes, keep the level of the water at the same height.

5. Draw a picture of your carrot plant every week. Keep the pictures together to make a book that shows its growth.

Questions:
1. Did any of your plants develop a leaf system?
2. Describe the differences between the leaf systems.
3. Did any of your plants develop a root system?
4. One type of root system has a single primary root from which other small roots grow. Which of your plants looks more like this type of system?
5. Anther type of root system has a branching system of roots that has many roots from which smaller roots develop. No single root becomes more important than others. Which of your plants looks like this type of system.
6. The roots in both of your plants arise because some roots give rise to more roots very easily. Since the roots developed at many places in both the sweet potato and the carrot, and since they are not leaves, what part of the plant do we eat when we eat sweet potatoes and carrots?

What Is the Function of Stems?

Purpose:
- Describe the function of the stem in plants.
- Observe what happens when water is drawn through carnation stem.

Materials Needed:
fresh white carnation
4 small test tubes
rubber band

Exacto knife (for adult use only)
4 colors of food coloring
clean milk carton

colored carnation flowers (dyed or grown)

Procedure:
1. For young students, slit the carnation stems ahead of time and place them back in water.
2. Show the students real flowers that have been colored and ask them to explain why carnations can be purple, blue, orange, or any color they wish.
3. Have students make predictions about how a florist "creates" or "makes" colored carnations. Some carnations such as red and pink are grown. However, carnations that are tinted colors or have the edges of the carnation colored are created using either a spray or coloring treatment using dyes.
4. See the student lab sheet for further instructions.

Answer Key For Questions:
1. Answers will vary. For example, the white petals will change color after the water is drawn through the stem of the plant.
2. Answers will vary. For example, each part of the flower will change to the color of the water that the stem has been placed in.

Behind the Scenes:
This activity will take a little bit of time before the students see results. Additionally, plant stems should be cut in water and placed in the test tubes as quickly as possible in order to prevent air from being drawn up into the stem.

Literature Links:
Butterfield, M. *Flower.* Simon & Schuster, 1991.
Ehlert, L. *Planting a Rainbow.* Harcourt Brace Jovanovich, 1988.
Ford, M. *Sunflower.* Greenwillow, 1995.
Kalman, B. *How a Plant Grows.* Crabtree, 1997.

Portals for Expansion:
Science • Conduct this activity using celery stalks or Queen Anne's Lace.
- Obtain other fresh flowers (lilies, zinnias, and daffodils) and have the students dissect the flowers to identify other parts of the flower.
- Compare the parts of a flower to the parts of a person to find similarities and differences in their functions.
- Conduct an experiment using a carnation whose stem has not been cut into quarters to determine if the water will travel through the stem quicker.

Math • Measure the length of the stem of the plant and time how long it takes the colored water to reach the top. Graph the results of several plants to determine the relationship.

Art • Ask a florist to visit the classroom and explain how flowers are colored.
- Create a floral arrangement using complementary colors.
- Mix paints to create a color wheel using the primary and secondary colors.

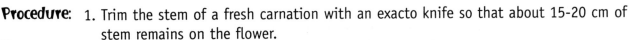

What Is the Function of Stems?

Procedure: 1. Trim the stem of a fresh carnation with an exacto knife so that about 15-20 cm of stem remains on the flower.
2. Quickly slice the bottom 5 cm of the remaining stem in half lengthwise, and then turn the stem a quarter-turn and slice it in half again, so that you have four quarters.
3. Wrap an elastic band around the four small test tubes and dispense a different colored dye into each tube, filling it about half full. Set the test tubes upright in the carton.
4. Make a hole in the lid of the carton. Insert the bottom of the stem through this hole and carefully insert each quarter of the stem into a different test tube. Place the lid on the carton to support the flower while the experiment is in progress.
5. It takes about half an hour for the dyes to rise to the petals. After this experiment has started answer the following questions:

   • Describe and illustrate what do you think will happen if a carnation stem is put into colored water?
   • Describe and illustrate what do you think will happen if a carnation stem is cut into four parts and then placed in four different colored waters?

6. Watch for changes in the flower and then draw pictures to show what happens.

Time Lapse	Observations/Illustrations
5 minutes	
15 minutes	

Time Lapse	Observations/Illustrations
30 minutes	
45 minutes	

Looking at Leaves

Purpose:
- Collect and classify leaves from at least ten trees found in the neighborhood.
- Identify the leaves using a tree identification book.
- Construct a key for the identification of only the trees found in the neighborhood.

Materials Needed:
scrapbook
waxed paper
decoupage finishing liquid
school glue
paper
pencil

Introduction: Leaf collections are a common assignment in science classes. However, the collection that is being suggested here is not purely for the appreciation of diversity of leaves, which is most often seen as the activity objective. This grouping and classification activity focuses on trees in the student's own neighborhood.

Procedure: See student lab sheet for instructions.

Behind the Scenes: The initial identification of the leaves can easily be accomplished by using a dichotomous key such as the key in the book, Watts, M. T. (1963). *Master Tree Finder: The Nature Studies Guild*. Berkeley, CA. A dichotomous key is one in which each question must be answered either one way or another, with each answer leading to the next question. Eventually, the leaf is identified. This same structure can be used in an identification tree, with branches branching until the tree is identified at the end of the branch. It is recommended to feature *evergreen vs. broadleaf* as the first branch, *simple or compound* as the first branch in the broadleaf section, and then *alternate or opposite* as the next step in each broadleaf category (see illustration). Continue to build branches until each leaf is identified at the end of a branch.

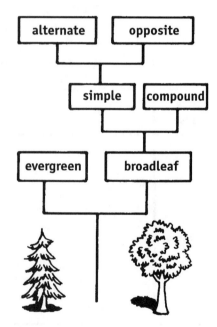

Decoupage finishing liquid is a specialized preservative available from most craft or hobby stores. When applied it will preserve each leaf specimen as well as adhere it on the page.

Literature Links:
Arnosky, J. Crinkleroot's *Guide to Knowing the Trees*. Bradbury Press, 1992.
Brooks, F. *Protecting Trees and Forests*. Scholastic, 1994.
Buscaglia, L. *The Fall of Freddie the Leaf*. Charles B. Slack, 1982.
Cartwright, M. *Usborne Conversation Guides: Protecting Trees and Forests*. Scholastic, 1991.
Ehlert, L. *Red Leaf, Yellow Leaf*. Harcourt Brace Jovanovich, 1991.
Heller, R. *Plants That Never Ever Bloom*. Scholastic, 1984.

Portals for Expansion:

Social Studies
- Conduct library research to find the different kinds of forests that occur in various geographic localities. Make an identification tree for those forests.
- Have each student find out the state tree is for the state in which he/she was born.

Art
- Invite a landscape architect to talk about the uses of trees in architecture.
- Using leaves or pieces of leaves, create a picture of a forest located in your region.

Language Arts
- Create a story about leaves after reading the picture book *Red Leaf, Yellow Leaf* in class.

Mathematics
- Estimate the height of a tree using the proportion consisting of the ratios of the length of a person's shadow to the length of the tree's shadow compared to the ratio of the height of that person to the unknown height of the tree. To do this: Measure the height of the person (A). Measure the length of his/her shadow (B). Measure the length of the tree's shadow (D). Multiply the height of the person times the length of the tree shadow, divide by the length of the person's shadow, and the height of the tree (C) is the result.

- Collect ten leaves of the same tree and measure their length and width. Use this information to plot a scattergram of the length vs width, and then calculate the average length and width of the tree.

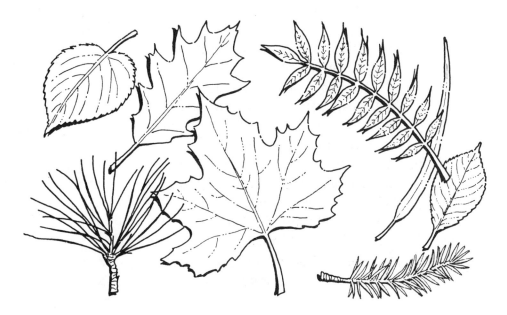

LAB
Plants

Looking at Leaves

Procedure:

1. Collect ten leaves from different trees in your neighborhood. Be sure at least two leaves are left on the twig when collected.

2. Record information about each leaf sample on the data sheet:
   - evergreen or broadleaf
   - simple (one leaflet per leaf) or compound (many leaflets per leaf)
   - leaves arranged on opposite sides of the twig or alternate from side to side
   - measure the leaf
   - draw a picture of the leaf

3. Using an identification key, identify each leaf by its common and scientific name.
4. Coat one side of the leaf with the decoupage liquid and let it dry.
5. Coat the other side of the leaf with decoupage liquid and use it to glue the leaf in a scrapbook.
6. Make a label with the common and scientific name of the tree from which the leaf was taken.
7. Glue that label on the page with the leaf.
8. Cover the page with waxed paper.

9. Repeat Steps 4–8 for each leaf sample. Continue until all ten leaves are mounted in the scrapbook. Close the scrapbook, then place several books or other heavy objects on it to hold the leaves flat as they dry.
10. Working in groups of three students, make an "identification tree" for the leaves collected. Begin with the tree branching into broadleaf trees and evergreen trees. Continue to branch your tree until all of your leaves are identified. See the diagram.

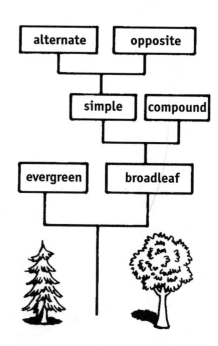

Looking at Leaves Data Sheet

	Evergreen or Broadleaf	Simple or Compound	Alternate or Opposite	Size in Centimeters	Draw a Picture
Leaf #1					
Leaf #2					
Leaf #3					
Leaf #4					
Leaf #5					
Leaf #6					
Leaf #7					
Leaf #8					
Leaf #9					
Leaf #10					

What Color of Light Helps Plants Grow?

Purpose:
- Recognize that some colors of light are more important for plant growth than others.
- Draw pictures and label plant parts that are affected by different colors of light.

Materials Needed:
bean seeds (lima or bush beans)
8 large drinking cups
clear plastic bag
colored cellophane (red, green, blue)
rubber bands
potting soil
water
pencils

Procedure: See student lab sheet for instructions.

Answer Key For Questions:
1. No
2. The one under the clear dome grew the best.
3. The plant under the red dome grew poorly.
4. Answers will vary. For example: plants need light to grow properly. If no light reaches that area in space, plants cannot produce their own food for continued growth.
5. Answers will vary. For example, some pollution may block out certain frequencies of light which plants need to grow.

Literature Links:
Ehlert, L. *Planting a Rainbow*. Harcourt Brace Jovanovich, 1988.
Gibbons, G. *From Seed to Plant*. Holiday House, 1991.
Heller, R. *Plants That Never Ever Bloom*. Scholastic, 1984.
Heller, R. *The Reason for a Flower*. Scholastic, 1983.
Kalman, B. *How a Plant Grows*. Crabtree, 1997.
Nelson, J. *How Does My Garden Grow?* Modern Curriculum Press, 1990.
Primavera, E. *Plantpet*. G. P. Putnam's Sons, 1994.
Relf, P. *The Magic School Bus: Plants Seeds*. Scholastic, 1995.

Portals for Expansion:
Science
- Repeat this activity using germinating seeds placed under different colors of light (as in the *Monocot and Dicot? What Is the Difference?* activity) to find out if a particular color of light affects the germination process.

Social Studies
- Research the topic of air pollution to find out if, and what kind of, sunlight can be blocked by air pollution.
- Invite a forest ranger to speak to the class about the kinds of plants in the forest and the importance of the forest biome as it grows from youth to maturity.
- Research how plants in different geographic or climate zones adapt to environmental conditions.

Language Arts
- Write a creative story that includes the parts of a seed and the process of germination.

Art
- Take the students on a rainbow hike. Give each student a colored square of paper. The student is then challenged to find that color as it appears in nature.

What Color of Light Helps Plants Grow?

Procedure:
1. Using a pencil, punch small holes in the bottoms of four cups.
2. Fill each cup three-quarters full with potting soil. Lightly pack the soil. Add water so that the soil is moist but not wet.
3. Place one bean seed, standing on end, into each cup.
4. Cover each cup with a plastic bag, and secure it with a rubber band.
5. Set aside and watch for plant growth.
6. When the tiny plants just start to emerge from the soil, remove the plastic bags.
7. Make covers for these cups by covering the remaining plastic cups with red, green, and blue cellophane or plastic wrap. Make one cover in each color. Keep one cup clear.
8. Measure and record the height of each plant.
9. Place the cover on each cup.
10. In four days, measure the height of the sprouts. Place the covers back on the plants as soon as the measurements are completed.
11. Continue the experiment to fill in the chart.

Color of Cover	4 days	7 days	11 days	14 days	17 days	21 days
Clear						
Red						
Blue						
Green						

Questions: *Answer the questions on the back of the paper.*
1. Do all of the plants grow at the same rate?
2. Which of your plants grew the best?
3. Did a plant seem to grow poorly under a certain color of cellophane?
4. Why would it be difficult to grow plants in deep space?
5. Does this discovery have any meaning if pollution were to block out certain kinds of sunlight?

How Does Your Garden Grow?

Purpose:
- Pant bean seeds and make observations about their growth.
- Observe plant structures such as the roots, leaves, stem, as a seed germinates.

Materials Needed:
resealable plastic bag
paper towels
water
potting soil or dirt
5-6 beans (lima, pinto, other store varieties)
soaking solution
variety of seeds (pumpkin, sunflower, etc)

Introduction: This activity can be tied into *What Does Your Garden Need to Grow?* since it requires the same materials. In this activity, students are making observations about the germination of seeds.

Setup:
1. Before planting, soak the beans for a few hours in a mixture of 1 liter of water to 15 mL bleach. *Note:* Bleach prevents mold from growing.
2. Plant some seeds in the soil and allow them to germinate. Watch for roots and stems to begin to grow. Do not let the stem break the soil. You want it as it exits the seed coat and begins to "right" itself in the soil. Remove from the soil and set aside for later observation.

Procedure:
1. Give each student a collection of seeds (pumpkin, sunflower, bean, corn,). Have the students to tell what the seeds have in common.
2. Ask the students to describe what they think the inside of a seed looks like.
3. Distribute seeds that have been soaked.
4. Have each student carefully split the bean along the seam in the seed coat and examine the seed parts. *Note:* Beans that have been soaked can be easily split with a fingernail. Also give the students seeds you have germinated for observations. What does each student notice about the parts of the seed once it has started to germinate? Have students record their observations on the back of the student lab sheets.
5. See the student lab sheet for further instructions. It works start extra plants for the next activity, *What Does Your Garden Need to Grow?*

Behind the Scenes: You will need to add water every few days to keep the paper towels moist. Do not let the students seal the plastic bags. Plants need the ability to exchange carbon dioxide in the air with the oxygen they produce.

Answer Key For Questions:
1. Answers will vary. For example, the sprout emerged first. This will vary depending on the direction of the seed's orientation when planted.
2. Answers will vary.
3. Answers will vary.

Literature Links:
Butterfield, M. *Flower*. Simon & Schuster, 1991.
Carle, E. *The Tiny Seed*. Picture Book Studio, 1987.
Dowden, A. O. *From Flower to Fruit*. Thomas Y. Crowell, 1984.
Ehlert, L. *Planting a Rainbow*. Harcourt Brace Jovanovich, 1988.
Ford, M. *Sunflower*. Greenwillow, 1995.
Gibbons, G. *From Seed to Plant*. Holiday House, 1991.
Kalman, B. *How a Plant Grows*. Crabtree, 1997.

Portals for Expansion:

Math
• Measure the increase in growth each day and graph the results showing the rate of increase against time.

Science
• Invite a greenhouse operator to your class to discuss how his work is different from farmers.

Social Studies
• Read about Biosphere II in Arizona and report on how plants were important to that project and the problems that occurred.

Language Arts
• Write a descriptive paragraph about what the was observed as the plants began to grow.

Art
• Clip advertisements from magazines that feature plants. Identify the kinds of plants shown. Create a collage with the pictures.
• Create a cartoon strip that tells the story of how a plant germinates and then grows.

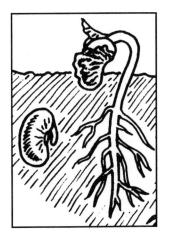
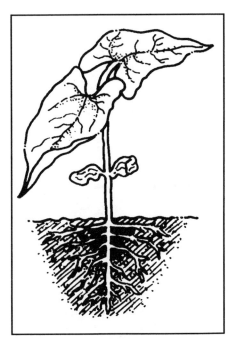

How Does Your Garden Grow?

Procedure:
1. Fold a paper towel into quarters and place it in the plastic bag so that the folded edge of the towel is along the bottom of the plastic bag.
2. In between the folds of the paper towel, place about 237 mL (1 cup) of soil.
3. Add water so the paper towel is damp.
4. Place beans in between the side of the plastic bag and the paper towel so that they are not touching each other.
5. Record your observations.

Day	Observations	Illustrations
1		
3		
5		
7		
_____		
_____		

Questions: *Answer the questions on the back of the paper.*
1. What did you first notice about the seed when it began to germinate?
2. What direction was the plant facing when it began to emerge from the seed coating?
3. Describe the changes that occurred once the plant broke through the surface of the soil?

What Does Your Garden Need to Grow?

Purpose: • Determine what conditions are needed for plants to grow.

Materials Needed:
bean seedlings
water
potting soil or dirt
5-6 beans (lima, pinto, other store varieties)
shoe boxes
milk cartons

Introduction: Read either *The Plant Sitter* by Zion or *Plantpet* by Primavera as an introduction to this activity. Since the students have already started growing their seeds as part of *How Does Your Garden Grow?* they will be anxious to determine what conditions are required to maintain healthy plants. To study these conditions, have the students remove some seedlings from the plastic bags and replant them in the milk cartons.

Procedure:
1. Discuss what a plant needs to live? Record the answers.
2. Engage the students in a discussion regarding how many or how much of each item a plant must have in order to survive. Follow up by asking if this is the same for all types of plants.
3. See student lab sheet for further instructions.
4. Using the chart provided, have students make and record observations about each of their four plants for two weeks.

Answer Key For Questions:
1. Answers will vary. For example, the plant in carton #3 grew the best because it received sunlight and an appropriate amount of water.
2. Answers will vary.

Literature Links:
Kalman, B. *How a Plant Grows*. Crabtree Publishing Company, 1997.
Primavera, E. *Plantpet*. G. P. Putnam's Sons, 1994.
Zion, G. *The Plant Sitter*. Harper and Row, 1959.
See bibliography on page 33 for additional titles.

Portals for Expansion:
Science
• Gather a variety of different plants, cactus, ivys, flowering plants, etc., and conduct this experiment again.
• Collect a variety of seed packages for gardens. Have students compare the information given regarding when to plant, how to plant, etc. Find out why certain plants grow better in rows than mounds, or why some plants are "cool season" crops and others need hot weather.
Social Studies
• Connect this activity with the activity *Who Grow What?* and have students depict on a map of their country the location of prime growing conditions for different types of crops. Have students discuss these terms or events: "The Corn Belt," "The Rice Bowl," "The Sun Belt," and "The Dust Bowl." Also discuss what impact or effect these areas have on plant growth and crop production in the United States.
Math
• Determine the ratio of plants that survive each type of growing conditions.

What Does Your Garden Need to Grow?

Procedure:
1. Cut the tops off of four clean milk cartons leaving about 10 cm in height.
2. Poke holes in the bottom of each carton to allow water to drain.
3. Replant two bean plants in each carton.
4. Label each milk carton with the variables the plant will receive.
   - Milk carton #1:   No water and no sunlight
   - Milk carton #2:   Water but no sunlight.
   - Milk carton #3:   Water and sunlight.
   - Milk carton #4:   Saturate with water and sunlight.
5. Place cartons 1 and 2 under a shoe box.
6. Place carton 3 and 4 in direct sunshine. Keep the soil in Carton #4 very wet by watering it each day.
7. Make observations every day or two and record them on the chart.

	Carton #1	Carton #2	Carton #3	Carton #4
Day _____				
Day _____				
Day _____				
Day _____				
Day _____				
Day _____				

Questions:
1. Describe which plant grew best. Under what conditions did the plant grow?
2. In the beginning of the experiment, all plants were growing. Which plant was the first to physically change? What were the changes?

Monocot or Dicot? What Is the Difference?

Purpose:
- Explain the differences between the germination of monocot and dicot seeds by conducting the activity.
- Make observations about a "monocot" and a "dicot" based on the shape of each germinating seed and the germination process.

Materials Needed:
clear plastic jar
paper towels
corn seed
lima bean seed
water

Introduction: Lima bean and corn seeds have different structures that vary in basic ways. Corn is a monocot, a relative of the grasses, while the lima bean is a dicot. The *mono-* and *di-* refer to the number of cotyledons, or seed leafs, that are a part of the germinating seed. The process of germination will be different for these two kinds of seeds and is important to recognize. This activity will allow the students to observe the differences clearly.

Procedure: See student lab sheet for instructions.

Behind the Scenes: The seeds to be used in this activity can be obtained from any garden center. Check the germination date on the package for freshness.

Answer Key For Questions:
1. Dicot (lima bean seed)
2. Monocot (corn seed)
3. Monocots germinate leaves with a cotyledon whereas dicots germinate leaves with a stem in the development of a dicot loop.

Literature Links:
Aliki. *Corn Is Maize: The Gift of the Indians.* Harper Collins, 1976.
Butterfield, M. *Flower.* Simon & Schuster, 1991.
Ehlert, L. *Planting a Rainbow.* Harcourt Brace Jovanovich, 1988.
French, V. *Oliver's Vegetables.* Orchard, 1995.
Gibbons, G. *From Seed to Plant.* Holiday House, 1991.
Heller, R. *The Reason for a Flower.* Scholastic, 1983.
Kalman, B. *How a Plant Grows.* Crabtree Publishing, 1997.
Relf, P. *The Magic School Bus: Plants Seeds.* Scholastic, 1995.

Social Studies
- Invite a local farm operator to speak to your class about the different ways crops grow and about supplying them for sale to the society.
- Research the kinds of crops raised in different areas of your country or the world.

Mathematics
- Measure the height of each germinating seed, from root tip to the end of the seed leaves, and graph the growth over the time of the activity.

Portals for Expansion:

Language Arts
• Write to a seed supplier to request information about the kinds of seeds that are offered for sale and their classification.
• Read the Laura Ingals Wilder books to determine the importance of seeds and crops at that time in history.

Art
• Create abstract mosaic pictures using different types of seeds as the medium.

Science
• Obtain seeds other than those used in the activity and determine if they are monocots or dicots.

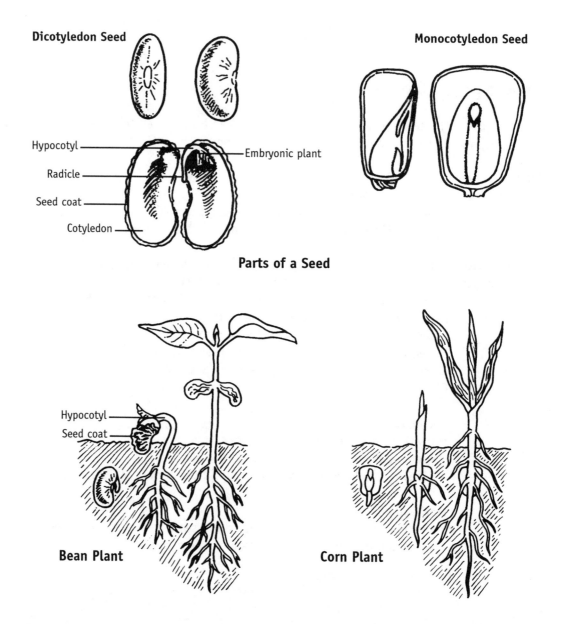

Dicotyledon Seed

Monocotyledon Seed

Hypocotyl — Embryonic plant
Radicle
Seed coat
Cotyledon

Parts of a Seed

Hypocotyl
Seed coat

Bean Plant

Corn Plant

Monocot or Dicot?
What Is the Difference?

Procedure:
1. Fold paper towels so that they fit inside a jar.
2. Put the paper towels against the inside of the jar.
3. Moisten the towels with water.
4. Put crumpled paper towels in the jar so that the folded paper towels stay against the sides of the jar.
5. Put three corn seeds and three bean seeds between the folded paper towels and the inside of the jar.
6. Keep the paper towels moist, but not soggy.
7. Observe the seeds for 15 days. Record your observations by drawing pictures.

	Day 3	Day 6	Day 9	Day 12	Day 15
Corn Seed					
Bean Seed					

Questions: *Answer the questions on the back of the paper.*
1. Which kind of seed has two seed leaves or cotyledons?
2. Which kind of seed has only one cotyledon?
3. What differences did you notice when these seeds germinated?

 IF8480 *Life Science*

Growing Mold

Purpose:
- Recognize bread mold as a form of plant life by growing it in an activity.
- Explain what conditions are necessary for bread mold to form by observing activity results.
- Describe that mold spores are a common part of our environment by collecting them to begin the activity.

Materials Needed:
bread (no preservatives)
3 resealable plastic bags
spray bottle with water
dark place for storage
A-V marker or china marker
tape

Introduction: Fungi is a large division of nonvascular plants. Many people recognize that fungi includes puff-balls and mushrooms. While some mushrooms are edible, most are not. What most people do not realize is that fungi includes molds. Bread mold is a common form of fungi growing on the occasional "bad bread." In this activity, the students will collect mold spores from their class-room using pieces of bread. They will discover that mold develops more quickly in a dark, moist environment. *Note:* It is important to stress that mold can cause health reactions for some peo-ple. The students will understand the health risks because the growing mold must never be exposed to the atmosphere in order to limit the dispersion of spores and allergic reactions that could result. Care must be taken to keep the plastic bags closed from the beginning of the activity until they are discarded.

Procedure: See student lab sheet for instructions.

Answer Key For Questions:
1. Answers will vary. For example, The moist bread which was placed in the dark produced the most mold.
2. The dry piece of bread which was placed in the light had the most mold growth.
3. Answers will vary but should include darker areas with moist conditions.
4. Shadows
5. Answers will vary. For example, the best conditions may include moist areas with darkness.

Literature Links:
Heller, R. *Plants That Never Ever Bloom.* Scholastic, 1984.
Relf. P. *The Magic School Bus: Plants Seeds.* Scholastic, 1995.

Portals for Expansion:

Language Arts/Science
- Research the topic of fungi and write a report about the various kinds of fungi and com-mercial uses.

Social Studies
- Interview a college researcher who can tell how fungi is more of a problem in warm, moist climates than it is in temperate and cold climates.

Health
- Interview a physician who can identify how fungi is a health concern in our society.

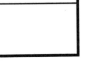

Growing Mold

Procedure:

1. Using a slice of bread, wipe dust from surfaces around the classroom.
2. Cut the dusty bread into three pieces. Wet one piece with a light spray of water. It should not be soggy, just moist.
3. Using a permanent marker, label three plastic bags with your name.
4. Write the word "light" on one bag, "dark" on another bag, and "dark moist" on the third bag.
5. Place the plain pieces of dusty bread into the first two bags. Seal the bags.
6. Place the moist bread into the third bag which is labeled "dark moist." Seal the bag.

7. Tape the bags to secure the sealed openings to remind you not to open them.
8. Place the "light" bag on a shelf where it is exposed to light.
9. Set the "dark" and "dark moist" bags in a drawer or closet that should remain closed except for observations.
10. Carefully wash your hands after completing this activity.
11. On the chart below, record daily observations for five days.

Day	Dry Bread in the Light	Dry Bread in the Dark	Moist Bread in the Dark
1			
2			
3			
4			
5			

Questions: *Answer the questions on the back of the paper.*

1. Which piece of bread had the most mold growth?
2. Which piece of bread had the least mold growth?
3. What conditions seem to favor the growth of mold?
4. Are you more likely to find fungi growing in the sunlight or in the shadows?
5. If you were a mushroom grower, what conditions would you provide to grow your product for stores?

Is Your Soil the Best Or Is Mine?

Purpose:
- Define clay, silt, sand, and humus in terms of its physical appearance and characteristics by closely inspecting each sample during the activity.
- Determine which material can allow water to pass through more easily by observing the activity. Determine which material can hold more water.
- Create a soil with a water holding ability equal to its ability to let water pass through by evaluating the activity results and testing a mixture based on those results.

Materials Needed:

china marker or A-V pen	water
five 470-mL (16-oz.) plastic drinking cups	stopwatch
graduated cylinder	sharp pencil
sand, silt, clay, and humus soil samples	permanent marker
six 240-mL (8-oz.) plastic drinking cups	magnifying lense

Introduction: The water holding ability of soil is an important characteristic. For a good rate of plant growth, the soil around a plant's roots must be able to hold water while being able to drain and not become soggy. Too much water or not enough water near the plant's roots will cause them to die. It is the relationship of sand, silt, clay, and humus that creates the ability of soil to let water pass through and to hold water in it. This activity asks which soils are best at holding water, which soils are best at allowing water to pass through, and then challenges the teams of students to create a mixture that holds as much water as it allows to pass through the soil.

Procedure:
1. Be sure the bottom of the 470 mL cup fits inside the 240 mL cup. The small sized cup is used for collecting the water that drains from the soil.
2. See student lab sheet for instructions.

Behind the Scenes: Samples of sand, clay, silt, and humus can be obtained from your local garden store without concern for the contents of the materials. Sand, clay, silt, and humus gathered from the environment may contain foreign materials which may not be healthy. Packaged materials will limit that concern.

Literature Links:
Bolwell, L., & Lines, C. *Where Plants Grow*. Wayland Publishers Limited, 1983.
Ford, M. *Sunflower*. Greenwillow Books, 1995.
Gibbons, G. *From Seed to Plant*. Holiday House, 1991.
Kalman, B. *How a Plant Grows*. Crabtree Publishing, 1997.
Kroll, S. *The Biggest Pumpkin Ever*. Holiday House, 1984.
Stevens, J. R. *Carlos and the Squash Plant*. Northland Publishing, 1993.

Portals for Expansion:
Mathematics
- Construct a line graph showing the differences in the time necessary for each cup to yield 120 mL of water.

Science
- Discuss why percolation rates are important if ground water becomes polluted.

Social Studies
- Invite a zoning officer to speak to the class about permits for on-site sewage systems and percolation tests. Report on the difference in permeability of soils between regions.

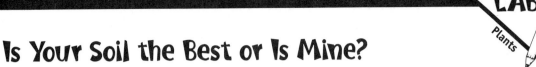

Is Your Soil the Best or Is Mine?

Procedure:
1. Collect 5 large plastic cups (470 mL). Carefully punch holes into the bottom of each one using a sharp pencil.
2. Fill each cup about half way with material:
   - Cup 1: Fill the cup with sand. Label the cup "sand."
   - Cup 2: Fill the cup with clay. Label the cup "clay."
   - Cup 3: Fill the cup with silt. Label the cup "silt."
   - Cup 4: Fill the cup with humus. Label the cup "humus."
   - Cup 5: Set the cup aside for use later.
3. Record what you observed about each material. Describe how each material feels, smells, and looks.

Sand	Clay	Silt	Humus

4. Carefully stack the cup with sand on top of small plastic cup.
5. Repeat Step 4 with each cup of material.
6. Fill a 240 mL cup with water.
7. Using a stopwatch or clock with a second hand, start timing when the water is dumped into the container with the sand.
8. After three minutes, use the china marker or grease pencil to mark the level of the water in the lower cup.
9. Repeat Steps 6–8 with each cup of material.
10. Rank the materials from 1 to 4 as to which soil **lets water pass** through it.
    (Write the numeral 1 on the cup which allows the most water to pass through the soil.)

11. Rank the materials from 1 to 4 as to which soil **holds more water.**
    (Write the numeral 1 on the cup which holds the most water.)

12. Record your results on the chart by writing the name of the material in the space:

	Holds Water	**Water Passes Through**
Most		
Second		
Third		
Least		

Finding the Perfect Soil

13. Using the results from your investigation, consider which materials would hold exactly half of the water (120 mL) poured into it.
14. Decide with a partner what proportion of sand, clay, silt, and humus to put into the fifth large plastic cup.

Sand	**Clay**	**Silt**	**Humus**

15. Fill the 240 mL cup with water. Repeat the investigation by repeating Steps 7 and 8.
16. Using a graduated cylinder, measure the water collected in the cup. How much water drained through the soil? _____
17. Try a different proportion of materials if the test was unsuccessful.

Questions:
1. How close were you to allowing exactly 120 mL of water to pass through the soil?
2. If you tried this investigation again, what ratio of materials would you use in your second soil mixture?
3. What proportion of materials do you think works the best?

Name That Plant!

Teacher Demonstration

Purpose:
- Identify a variety of outdoor plants with the help of the teacher.
- Sketch plants that fall into different categories.

Materials Needed:
drawing paper
colored pencils
wooded area for nature walk
field guides
resealable plastic bags

Introduction: One of the best ways to observe various types of plants is to take a nature walk in a wooded area or field. Providing students with opportunities to study plants in natural settings are worthwhile science experiences. It is suggested that the teacher prepare in advance by marking a short trail and identifying selected plants before working with the students.

Procedure:
1. Select an area to take a nature walk with your students.
2. Review the following nature walk rules with the class before venturing into the outdoors.
   - Students should be very careful not to disturb any living creatures (bugs included).
   - Students should not attempt to catch any living creatures such as snakes, frogs, and salamanders.
   - Students should not eat any berries or other fruits and nuts found outdoors.
   - Students should make observations with their eyes and not destroy or kill any of the plants.
3. Have each student place colored pencils and drawing paper into a plastic bag for the investigation.
4. Stop along an identified path and point out different types of plant life. It is important to explain to students what category each designated plant belongs:
   - vascular or nonvascular
   - seed bearing (gymnosperms) or non-seed bearing (angiosperms),
   - flower producing or non-flower producing
5. Allow students opportunities to investigate and observe these plant types.
6. Have students sketch the different types of plants, noting similarities and differences.
7. End the hike with a story or other activity related to plants.

Behind the Scenes: *Safety Note:* Teachers should be knowledgeable of the appearance of poison ivy, poison sumac, and poison oak. One of the benefits of showing students these plants is to help them recognize specific characteristics. Take time to carefully show students special plant features, such as the runners that certain plants send out to help populate an area, the spores on the underside of a fern leaf, and so on. These first-hand experiences will stay with students much longer than illustrations in books.

Literature Links:

Arnosky, J. *Crinkleroot's Guide to Knowing the Trees*. Bradbury Press, 1992.
Brooks, F. *Protecting Trees and Forests*. Scholastic, 1994.
Cole, J. *Plants in Winter*. Thomas Y. Crowell, 1973.
Ehlert, L. *Red Leaf, Yellow Leaf*. Harcourt Brace Jovanovich, 1991.
Heller, R. *Plants That Never Ever Bloom*. Scholastic, 1984.
Heller, R. *The Reason for a Flower*. Scholastic, 1983.
Kalman, B. *How a Plant Grows*. Crabtree, 1997.
Krudop, W. L. *Something Is Growing*. Atheneum, 1995.
Muller, G. *Around the Oak*. Dutton's Children's Books, 1994.
Overbeck, C. *How Seeds Travel*. Lerner Publications, 1982.

Portals for Expansion:

Science

- Repeat this activity in the winter and compare plants that still have leaves with those which do not.
- Have students make spore prints with the caps of mushrooms on different colored papers. Compare the results.
- Create leaf art with either crayon rubbings or prints using ink rollers to show the different vein structures in the leaves.

Language Arts

- Have student write Cinquain or Haiku poetry about the leaves and plants they observe.
- Ask students to close their eyes for five minutes and just listen to what is happening around them. Then have students write descriptive essays about what they heard.

Math

- Place a circle of rope or string on the ground and have students do a population count of the different types of plants found in the sample area. Have them construct graphs depicting the ratio of different types of plants in several sample areas.

Art

- Allow students to take their nature sketches and create personalized note cards or stationary with the pictures.

Social Studies

- Locate and observe plants that are native to the area in which you live.
- Determine what plants were important to Native American nations in your geographic region.

INVERTEBRATES

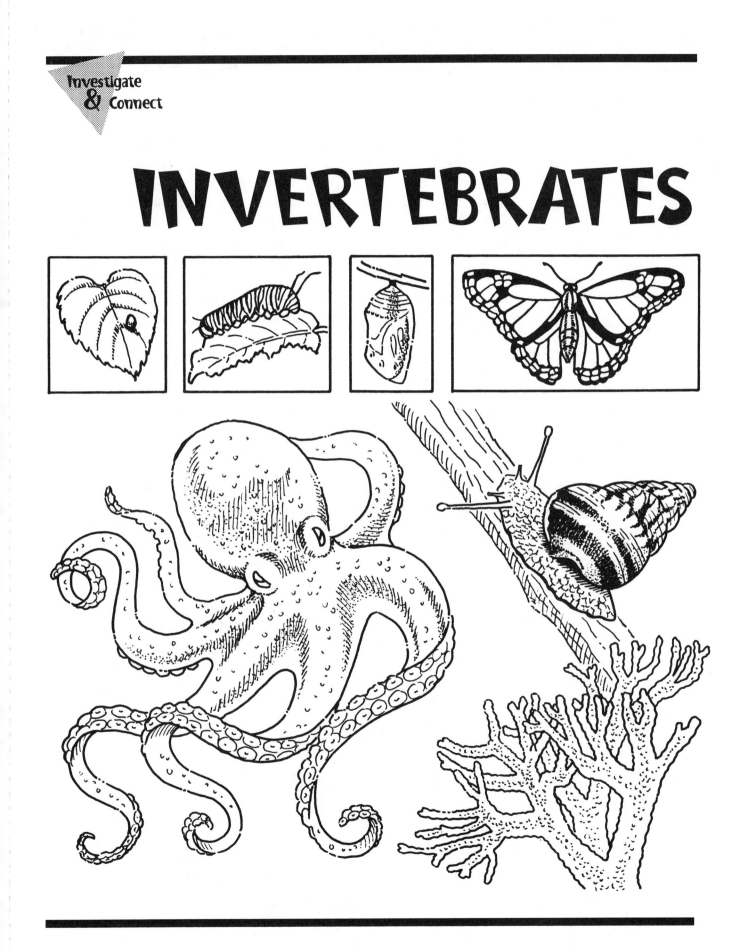

Fascinating Facts for Teachers

Invertebrates The animal kingdom is studied within the science of zoology. Zoology has found some basic differences between the animal and plant kingdoms. As a form of life, animals show the characteristics that all living things show, such as form and composition, metabolism (they demonstrate life processes), irritability (they react to stimuli), growth, and reproduction. However, animals differ from plants in that no animal can make its own food for metabolism, most animals can respond quickly, including locomotion in many cases, to stimuli due to a nervous system, and their delicate systems are usually internal. Although most students learn easily to recognize the difference between plants and animals, some life-forms can fool them. The Venus flytrap is a plant, although the trigger mechanism in its physiology will snap shut on an unsuspecting insect as if it had jaws and muscles. The coral, an animal, does not show locomotion once it takes residence in its anchored shell. These are some examples that seem to be contradictory and can be used in clarifying with students the differences between plants and animals.

See Portal for Exploration "Building an Animal Cell" The basic unit of structure in the animal is the cell. The similarities of the animal cell and the plant cell are many. The animal cell has several structures. The *nucleus* serves as the control center of the cell. *Mitochondria* serve together as the powerhouse of the cell. The chemical reactions that take place within each mitochondrion yields the energy that drives the life processes of the cell. The *endoplasmic reticulum* are systems of parallel structures that divide the cell into segments and provide routes of travel through the cell for a variety of materials. The *golgi bodies,* which are thought to function as a protein packaging factory, prepare proteins for export out of the cell. The *ribosomes,* the site of protein syntheses, create the material needed for growth and repair. Finally, the *vacuoles* act as the storage site for fluid and granular wastes. All of these structures are found within the cell, its borders defined by a membrane called the *cell membrane.* The semipermeable membrane allows for the selective passage of materials required for life processes but resists the exit of the structures which live inside a gelatinous fluid called *cytoplasm.*

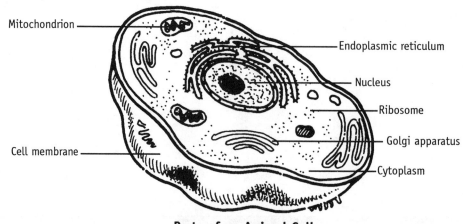

Mitochondrion

Endoplasmic reticulum

Nucleus

Ribosome

Golgi apparatus

Cell membrane

Cytoplasm

Parts of an Animal Cell

The typical animal cell differs from the typical plant cell in two very important ways. First, the animal cell does not have a cell wall. The plant cell wall provides structural rigidity to the cell which is provided by other means by the animal cell. Systems of skeletons or shells take the place of the function served by cell walls in plants. Another significant difference is the absence of chloroplasts which are present in all green plant cells. Chlorophyll is the material that assists plants in the conversion of light energy from the sun into energy that is needed to drive the process of photosynthesis. As we all know, animals do not carry on photosynthesis and cannot make their own foods, so they must eat to provide that energy. Thus, the structures that serve the function of driving photosynthesis are absent from animal cells.

Many cells may serve similar functions and together make up tissues. Tissues may differentiate into epithelial (or covering) tissues, connective and supporting tissues (including circulatory), muscular, and nervous tissues. Epithelial tissues cover the organism against the outside and protect the organs if the outside penetrates the organism, as in the protection offered as part of the digestive system. Connective and supportive tissues bind the organism together in a number of ways. Some of this tissue forms intercellular substances holding cells together, and some actually form fibers holding cells together. Vascular tissues, a type of supportive tissue, transport and distribute fluids throughout the organism. This includes both the circulation of blood and lymph. Muscular or contractile tissues are capable of causing movement in the parts to which the muscles are attached. There are a variety of classifications of muscles including striated as in the biceps, nonstriated, as in the muscle of the digestive system, and cardiac muscle of the heart. Nervous tissues transmit electrical impulses that carry senses and initiate movement. The nerve cell has two ends, the dendrite that brings electrical impulses to the nerve cell, and the axon that carries the electrical impulse away from the cell.

In organisms, tissues from organ systems serve important functions within the organism. Most of the invertebrates and all of the vertebrates have these systems, although in some of the invertebrates, the functions may not use a separate organ system. The functions include the organism's body covering, the skeletal system, the muscular system, the circulatory system, the digestive system, the respiratory system, the excretory system, the endocrine system, the nervous system, and the reproductive system.

As the variety of animal life is reviewed, reference will be made to the organ systems and how that animal's organ system functions to meet its needs. The kingdom is broken down into the phylum, class, order, family, genus, and species. Each animal known and classified can be specifically described using the Latin terms, genus and species. It is beyond this book to be that specific. So, this examination is cursory and will mention only several examples of the animals contained within each of the major divisions of the animal kingdom (phylum), and also, when necessary, the class (division of a phylum) will be discussed.

Headless Things

The first of the simple animals, or "lower animals," are represented here by those animals that do not have identifiable heads. These headless animals include the bacteria, protozoans, the porifera, and the coelenterates. The protozoans are mostly microscopic one-celled animals that live in the ocean, freshwater bodies, or in moist, decaying material. They all live in some version of a wet environment, including the bodies of plants and other animals. Bacteria, in some texts, is placed into a different kingdom of life, the Monerans. If classified this way, they would not be animals at all, but for the purposes of this discussion, they will be considered as animals. Bacteria live in a wide range of environments from terrestrial forms to aquatic forms, and from the heat of hot springs to the cold of the Arctic. Some bacteria even live in the moist throat of humans and cause an infection we know as "strep throat." Other bacterias serve constructive purposes as they live on rocks in trickle filters, a secondary treatment device in sewage treatment plants. Eschrica coli (E. coli) is a bacteria that can sicken or kill humans when ingested, although the organism serves an important function in the lower parts of the human digestive system.

See Portal for Exploration "Pond Residents"

Many other organisms are included in the protozoans. Every student who has taken high school biology knows the euglena, the paramecium, and the amoeba. The amoeba moves by extending its jelly-like protoplasm in one direction, and then drawing whatever is left toward the new position. It does not walk; rather, it flows into the new position. It eats by surrounding a piece of food with its protruded pseudopodia (or false arms) and then closing its entire body around the food. The food then becomes a part of the protoplasm as a vacuole that shrinks in size as the food is digested. The paramecium has the same shape, roughly, as the sole of a shoe. It is covered with cilia that move to propel the organism through the water. The euglena is a long, thin, single-celled organism with one flagellum that has chlorophyll in chloroplasts. This shows how close these organisms are to the plant kingdom. Some biologists classify the protozoans as a separate kingdom—the protista.

Amoeba

Paramecium

Euglena

Protozoans

The phylum Porifera includes the sponge, a low form of multi-celled life. Its tiny body, together with others in its colony, secretes a shell that attaches to the rocky ocean bottom, thus rendering the animal incapable of locomotion. The colonies build shapes that range from nearly tree-like to large flat plates. The colors range from dull grey to brilliant orange, blue, yellow, and others. The sponge looks, in life, like a plant growing from the ocean floor. With its body removed, the skeleton of the sponge has commercial value as a tool for the bathroom or for use on your car. Sponges differ from the protozoans since there does exist some small degree of cell differentiation which forms a limited type of tissue.

See Portal for Exploration "Build a Coral Reef"

The phylum Cnidaria, also known as coelenterates, are the lowest animals with clearly differentiated tissues and structures. All of the creatures live in water, and most in the ocean. They live in one of two forms; the polyp has a tubular body with one end closed and the other having a central mouth. The medusa is an umbrella-shaped gelatinous mass with tentacles along the outer edge and a mouth in the center, mounted on a protrusion on the concave inner surface of the umbrella shape. This group of animals includes the hydra, jellyfish, sea anemones, and corals. The range in size of the animals is great, with hydra from 10 mm long to the giant man-of-war that may reach 10 meters (11 yards) in length.

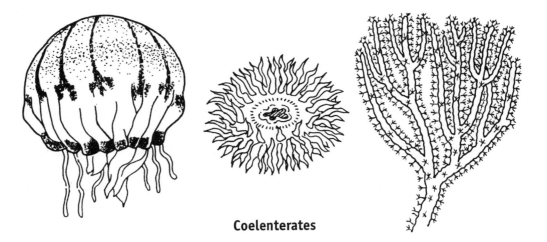

Coelenterates

Floaty Things

The following phyla are those that are usually found in marine environments: the echinoderms, the molluscs, and the brachiopoda. They may have freshwater or terrestrial forms, but they are more recognized for their existence in the realm of deep ocean waters. The brachiopods were much more common in the oceans of geologic time, ranging to nearly a meter in width. Many of them persist today but as much smaller animals, 1–7 cm in size, in the world's oceans. The brachiopod's bivalve shell is attached to the ocean floor by a fleshy stalk. The creature has many organ systems developed in its soft body: a well developed nervous system, a digestive system, a small heart, and a sexual reproductive system.

The echinoderms are well known because of one of its classes, the sea stars. This phylum also contains the feather stars, the brittle stars, the sea urchins, and sea cucumbers. These animals show radial symmetry in five parts with a spiny covering. All of these creatures are marine; they have digestive tracts, tiny structures that serve the function of locomotion, and sexual reproductive systems. Every child recognizes the sea star (also called the starfish), but not many know that it is a well-developed creature. Some starfish are very harmful to their own habitats as they consume the coral reefs which serve as their homes. Fishermen often cut the stars in half in an effort to destroy them and save the coral reefs. Each of the starfish halves merely regenerate the missing half, forming two starfish from that which was one, doubling the original problem.

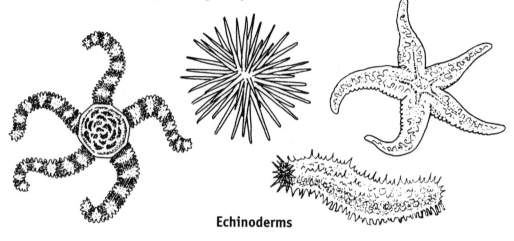

Echinoderms

See Portal for Exploration "The Test Tube Aquarium"

The molluscs are found, usually, in fresh- and saltwater, but some are found on land. A mollusc usually has a soft body covered by a shell that has been secreted by the animal. The shell is coiled in some species and non-existent in a few species, such as the land-based slug, enemy of all gardeners. It has an identifiable head and a foot consisting of a strong muscle that serves the purpose of locomotion. Each mollusc has a complete digestive tract, circulatory system, heart, nervous system, and sexual reproductive system. This phylum includes the clam and its relatives, squid, octopus, snail, abalone, and nautilus.

See Portal for Exploration "The Case of Mistaken Identity"

Pelecypoda, a class within molluscs, also has a well-earned reputation. Pelecypods are used for food by humans, with the entire clam or oyster being eaten, raw or steamed. Humans eat only a single muscle of a scallop, often cut into flat cylinders. Oysters (and some other pelecypods) produce a material that coats any foreign material caught between the outer soft parts of the animal and the inside of its hard, protective shell. This coating has a lustrous sheen, and the objects, once coated, are called pearls. Whether the foreign object is purposely placed into the oyster creating a "cultured" pearl, or whether the irritating foreign object arrives as a natural accident, the results are the same.

Molluscs

Many stories abound among mariners of sea monsters that inhabit the deep, and many of these monsters are molluscs. Since before the fanciful travels of the submarine "Nautilus" in the novel *20,000 Leagues Under the Sea,* the giant squid has been portrayed as a terrible inhabitant of the deep. This may not be too untrue, since the giant squid is known to grow to an amazing 20 meters (22 yards) in length and is, as are all animals in its class (cephalopods), a predator.

Wiggly Things

There are two very different groups of worms to be addressed here: first, the simple (unsegmented) worms, and second, the segmented worms. Within the simple worm group are found the Platyhelminthes (flatworms) and the Nematoda (roundworms). The phylum Platyhelminthes' characteristics are described by its name. *Platy* means flat, and all of these simple worms are just that—flat. Interesting members of this phylum include the free-swimming "cross-eyed" worm called the planaria which shows excellent regeneration properties. If the planarian would be cut in half, each half would regenerate the other missing half. Each has eyespots which give the appearance of being "cross-eyed," a simple digestive tract and a simple nervous system; planarian usually have both sexes in one organism.

Also included in the phylum Platyhelminthes are the flukes, which are all parasitic. A disease of cattle and sheep can be caused by the sheep liver fluke, but the creature must live part of its life cycle in a particular snail. Most at risk, then, are livestock animals that use pastureland near, or including, wetlands that can serve as habitats for snails. A number of flukes are named for the organ systems they can attack in "higher" animals. The intestinal fluke, lung fluke, and blood fluke are found in various parts of the world. In some waters of the United States, the free-swimming cercaria (an animal that changes into a nonhuman fluke later in its life cycle) can cause swimmer's itch if it buries itself into the skin of an unsuspecting swimmers.

The tapeworms are also part of the flatworm phylum. They are parasitic worms with segment-like sections that grow from a "head." Most commonly known of these worms is the human tapeworm which grows inside the human intestine. This creature enters the human through improperly (under) cooked pork where a cyst may exist. Once the cyst enters the intestine, a "head" with suckers and hooks begins to grow, adding segment-like sections behind it. Tapeworms may have anywhere from none to 10 meters of segments behind the head.

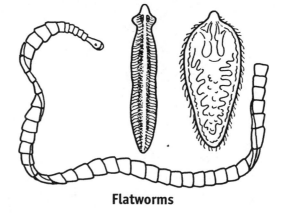

Flatworms

The phylum Aschelminthes include the nematodes and rotifers. The nematodes may range from the round worms that live in soils eating the organic material found there to parasitic forms that live in other animals. They differ from the flatworms due in their round form. They have complete digestive tracts, well-developed muscle fibers, and nervous systems. The sexes are usually separate. Ascaris is one roundworm that lives in many humans, especially in rural areas. The pork roundworm can be passed from young pig to young pig simply through the infected soil of a pig-yard. The rotifers are very small creatures. They range in size from microscopic to 1 mm. The rotifer's very attractive appearance is highlighted by a ring of beating cilia that appears to be a rotating disk. Each has a digestive tract, nervous system, and a reproductive system with separate sexes. The rotifers are an amazingly diverse group of simple animals that are a favorite of microscope users when looking at pond, lake, or other samples of standing water.

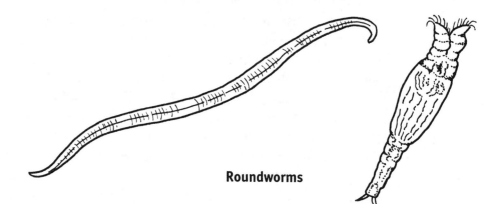

Roundworms

See Portal for Exploration "Life in the Soil"

The segmented worms are members of the phylum Annelida. The annelids are more advanced creatures than the unsegmented worms discussed earlier. They are obviously segmented, with a cuticle covering them in a moist coating. They have complete digestive tracts and nervous systems, and a circulatory system complete with a heart. This phylum include the earthworms, the marine worms found mainly near the shore, and the leeches. While most earthworms are only a few inches or less in length, some worms are larger. Marine worms of the Pacific Coast can grow to nearly 3 meters (10 feet). Leeches are usually small and in the order of 1 cm or smaller. However, some varieties can grow to 20 cm (8 in.) in length.

See Portal for Exploration "An Earthworm's Heartbeat"

See Portal for Exploration "Composting with Worms"

The earthworm is an important fish bait, and is said to be important in the production of fertile soil. The castings of earthworms may contribute to this process, but their burrows loosen the ground making it more prone to erosion. Earthworm burrows can also ruin irrigation ditches. However, the earthworm does aerate the soil, and this can be important where the soil is thin. However, rumors of increasing the quality of soil by adding earthworms are simply untrue.

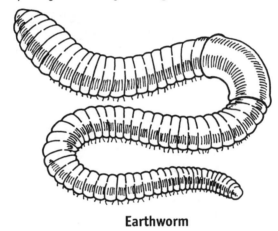

Earthworm

Leeches are small terrestrial or aquatic predators, scavengers, or parasites. Most leeches live in freshwater, and they move either by forming loops to move like inchworms, or they swim in an undulating movement. Although they may feed on small worms or insects, they may also feed on the dead remains of larger organisms. The leeches are best known, however, for those species that attach to animals and feed on blood drawn from the host. Most activity is nocturnal, but the leech can be active in the daytime, especially if food presents itself. A leech may feed by drawing several times its own weight of blood from its host; the blood yields sustenance as it decomposes within the animal over the next several months. The action of leeches was once thought to be of great medicinal value in a process known as "blood letting." Recent research is again investigating the effects of these creatures in the medical field.

Crawly Things

See Portal for Exploration "Create Your Own Insect"

The phylum Arthropoda contains the joint-footed animals. This includes some of the more well-known invertebrates such as the insects, crustaceans, and arachnids. The insects are, by far, the largest class of this phylum containing both the largest number of individuals and the largest number of species. An insect has a structure with three distinct body parts: the head, thorax, and abdomen. It also has one pair of antennae and mouthparts on the head, three pair of legs on the thorax, a complete digestive system, a simple circulatory system with a heart, a nervous system, and a reproductive system with separate sexes. While most have wings, some insects have two pair, some have one pair, and some have none. The sizes of the insects range from millimeters to the huge Venezuelan beetle that may reach 15 cm (6 in.) in length. The grasshopper is the animal usually used to show the features of most insects, since it clearly demonstrates most of the characteristics of insects.

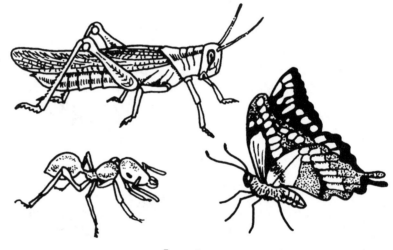

Insects

Most insects are solitary; that is, they live by themselves. Some insects, however, are social. They live assembled in large numbers. This behavior can most clearly be seen in the honeybee that lives in a system in which clear responsibilities are taken by different members of the social system, and survival of the whole, called a swarm, is based on the work of each individual in its social role. The queen lives in the hive and has the primary responsibility of laying eggs. Drones live to fertilize the eggs of new queens, and the workers provide all other functions of the society. They raise the young bees, gather and provide food for all in the swarm, and build and maintain the hive. They even direct other bees to nectar by doing a "dance" among the other bees that describes the direction of the nectar-rich source. This social system is protected by the workers through the use of their stingers, whether the threat comes from other bees trying to take the honey or from a hungry bear. This social behavior can also be seen in some other species of insects, including ants and termites.

Many insects are beneficial to humans. The honeybee is one example that produces, not only honey, but beeswax used in candles. Bees are also very important in the pollination process needed for the reproduction of some plants. As the bees collect nectar, they also carry pollen from one plant to the next, serving this most important function in the life cycle of plants. Another example of a beneficial insect is the silkworm. This insect larva produces a cocoon that contains about 300 meters (328 yards) of silk fiber. If 90,000 cocoons are unwound, enough fiber can be recovered to produce about one kilogram of silk thread. Some harmful insects are eaten by predacious insects. A host of beetles, flies, and wasps have been imported to control the numbers of harmful insects in a process known as "biologic control" of harmful pests.

Many harmful insects are not harmful as adults, but in the juvenile stages of their lives. Insects spend some time as juveniles in one of two forms. If the juvenile form of an insect looks much like the adult, such as the grasshopper, the juvenile form is called a nymph. The nymph simply sloughs off its exoskeleton, thus allowing room for growth, and then it secretes a new exoskeleton. If the juvenile form of the insect does not look like the adult, the juvenile is called a larva. The gypsy moth is a truly unremarkable plain-looking brown moth as an adult. Its larval stage is as a caterpillar with a voracious appetite for the leaves of deciduous trees. Between the larval stage and the adult, the creature changes form to become something it never looked like before. This change from larva to adult is a process called metamorphosis, a word with the Latin roots for changed (*meta*) and form (*morph*).

Some insects are harmful. Insect damage to crops amounts to billions of dollars each year. Important crops like corn and wheat have hundreds of potential enemies in the form of insects. The chinch bug, the potato beetle, and the grasshopper are native pests. Imported pests (imported by accident or by failed attempts at biological control) include the cotton boll weevil, the corn borer, and the Hessian fly which destroys wheat. Human food is ruined by cockroaches and houseflies. Wool clothing is ruined by moth larvae. Houses are damaged by the larvae of termites. Bedbugs cause allergies to blossom and mosquitoes can transmit diseases in humans. Efforts to control these harmful pests is a huge industry that has, in the past, significantly impacted the environment and the variety of life in that habitat. A notable example is the use of DDT that resulted in a biomagnification, as its effects were compounded in the food web and eventually caused the weakening of birds' eggshells and threatened the survival of many bird species.

The crustaceans contain shrimp, water fleas, barnacles, crayfish, crabs, and their relatives. Most are aquatic creatures but some, like the sow bug, live in moist soils. Many, like the crab, live as free swimming singular animals while others, like shrimp, swim in huge schools. Still others, like barnacles, live attached to objects such as rocks or as parasitic creatures attached to large animals, including the whale. The head has two pairs of antennae, a thorax, and an abdomen each made of sections. These sections may be visible on the thorax but are clearly visible on the abdomen. Crustaceans usually have "tails"; have complete digestive, muscular, and circulatory systems; use gills for respiration; and have separate sexes.

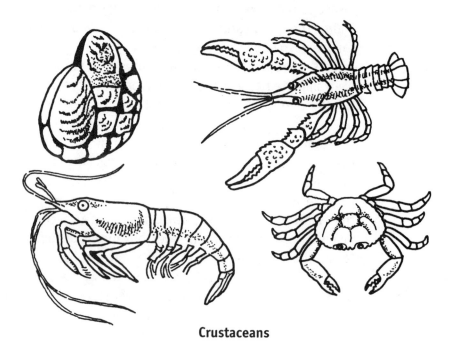

Crustaceans

Many crustaceans are prized as food. Shrimp are caught in huge nets towed behind powerful ships uniquely designed for the task. These creatures are also a mainstay in the marine food web, but large species, such as those from the warm waters of the Gulf of Mexico, are valued by the human species. Crabs of several species are also prized by that same predator. A particular importance is placed upon the meaty legs of the Alaskan "king" crab. Crabs are not caught in nets, instead they are lured into traps that are easy to enter but difficult for the creatures to leave. Crab traps and lobster pots are marked by buoys, color coded for ownership, all over the Chesapeake Bay and in the cold waters of the Northern Atlantic.

Not all crustaceans are welcome by humans. Barnacles grow on the sides of ships and interfere with the smooth flow of water around the hulls. This reduces the efficiency of the ship, and the buildup of barnacles can interfere with the operation of the moving parts of the submerged portions of the vessel. Sow bugs can attack plants in gardens. The crayfish can also weaken levees with their burrowing behavior. Some crustaceans burrow into the wood of docks and wharfs, and some crustaceans can act as intermediate hosts of human parasites.

See Portal for Exploration "Invert Inventory"
Arachnids include the spiders, scorpions, and ticks. They are, generally, terrestrial, and have four pairs of legs. The spider has a structure that consists of two rounded parts, the cephalothorax and abdomen, on which no segmentation can be observed. Spiders live as single predatory individuals eating insects as their main food. Spiders inject paralyzing poisons and digestive juices into their victims, thus beginning the process of digestion even before the victim is ingested. The hunting behaviors of spiders is an interesting study. Some spiders simply wait until their webs catch their prey, while others are active hunters and actually chase down their prey.

Scorpions are inhabitants of desert-like regions with warm temperatures and low humidities. The scorpion's body is long and slender with a segmented abdomen that terminates in a sharp poisonous sting. Scorpions live under rocks or in burrows and are capable of using the end of their long thin tails to sting their prey with paralyzing poisons. Their preys are then torn apart and eaten.

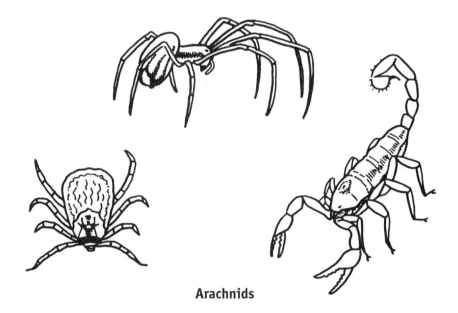

Arachnids

Ticks are small to microscopic in size with a head, thorax, and abdomen close together and unsegmented. The tick's usually slender mouthparts burrow under the skin to suck the blood of the host on which it lives. Adult ticks climb on bushes and trees and drop onto hosts as they pass nearby. Some ticks carry human diseases like Rocky Mountain spotted fever (no longer restricted to the Rocky Mountain region) or Lyme disease transmitted by the deer tick, usually in a bite that produces a large "bull's-eye." Some ticks can produce slow healing sores, so the best defense is an active offense. When "in the field," wear a hat covering the head and long pants. When returning from the field, a close examination should be made to insure that a tick has not found its mark.

Boyle, D. *Coral Reef Hideaway*. Soundprints, 1995.
This book tells the story of a clown anemonefish that lives among the tentacles of sea anemones and protects its young from other coral reef animals.

Broger, A. *The Caterpillar's Story*. Scroll Press, 1972.
An excellent book on metamorphosis, the reader is told in story form what happens as a caterpillar eats its way through the leaves, forms a cocoon, and eventually emerges as a butterfly.

Brown, R. *If at First You Do Not See*. Holt, Rinehart and Winston, 1982.
A rebellious caterpillar takes off on his own to find adventurer; however, he has some amazing encounters before he turns into a butterfly. The pictures in this book change as you turn the book sideways and upside down to read the words.

Brown, R. *Ladybug, Ladybug*. E. P. Dutton, 1988.
An extension of the old rhyme "ladybug, ladybug, fly away home," this book tells the journey of a ladybug that is blown from a young boy's hand as she attempts to get home."

Carle, E. *The Honey Bee and the Robber*. Scholastic, 1981.
The story tells about the problems a honeybee encounters as it attempts to gather nectar to make honey. The end of the book has page by page descriptions that tell the reader about the habits and behaviors of bees.

Carle, E. *The Very Busy Spider*. Scholastic, 1984.
A farm spider diligently spins her web despite the constant interruptions and diversions from the other animals.

Carle, E. *The Very Hungry Caterpillar*. Scholastic, 1987.
A caterpillar emerges from an egg and eats his way through a variety of fruits and other foods, then his body forms a cocoon, and later emerges as a butterfly. This easy reader is a good book to show the life cycle of a butterfly.

Carle, E. *The Very Quiet Cricket*. Philomel, 1990.
A tiny newborn cricket encounters other insects that make much more noise than he when they greet each other. The small cricket finds himself with another cricket and soon realizes that his sound will be louder.

Carle, E. *The Very Lonely Firefly*. Philomel, 1995.
A single firefly encounters many types of light at night as he searches for other fireflies. This easy reader is a good book to use when talking about individual characteristics of insects.

Cassie, B., & Pallotta, J. *The Butterfly Alphabet Book*. Charlesbridge Publishing, 1995.
Each letter of the alphabet portrays a specific butterfly or part of a butterfly in unique prose.

Cole, J. *The Magic School Bus on the Ocean Floor*. Scholastic, 1992.
Ms. Frizzle takes her students on a journey to the bottom of the ocean floor. On the way there, they encounter various creatures that live in the different levels of the ocean, such as zooplankton, algae, and molluscs.

Cole, J. *The Magic School Bus Inside a Beehive*. Scholastic, 1996.
Ms. Frizzle takes her class on a field trip to the inside of a beehive. While there, her students are able to observe the many characteristics of bees.

Cooney, H. *Underwater Animals*. Time Life Books, 1996.
This factual book provides vivid pictures and information about animals that live in a marine environment.

Craig, J. *Amazing World of Spiders*. Troll, 1990.
An excellent book, it discusses the behavior and characteristics of spiders.

DeLuise, D. *Charlie the Caterpillar*. Aladdin, 1990.
This affective story tells how a young caterpillar is shunned by other creatures until he progresses through metamorphosis and emerges as a butterfly.

Dorros, A. *Ant Cities*. Scholastic, 1987.
Explains in a very clear way the different roles ants take on within their cities. Provides illustrations that are labeled and explains additional information to the reader.

Edwards, P. D. *Some Smug Slug*. HarperCollins, 1996.
Through the use of alliteration, this story tells of a slug that, despite the warnings of creatures, finds himself eaten by a frog in the end.

Facklam, M. *Creepy, Crawly Caterpillars*. Little, Brown and Company, 1996.
Several species of caterpillars are introduced to the reader through a color illustration of each insect along with the stages of metamorphosis. The book gives information about each caterpillar and its ability to survive.

Fichter, G.S. *Bees, Wasps, and Ants*. Racine, Western Publishing, 1993.
A Junior Golden Guide book, it provides information and facts about bees, wasps, and ants. This is good reference material.

Fichter, G.S. *Butterflies and Moths*. Western Publishing, 1993.
This Junior Golden Guide book offers information and facts about butterflies and moths. It is a good reference resource for children.

Fichter, G.S. *Starfish, Seashells, and Crabs*. Western Publishing, 1993.
A Junior Golden Guide Book, it discusses starfish, seashells, and crabs, offering information and facts about the animals. This is good resource for children.

George, J. C. *The Moon of the Monarch Butterflies*. Thomas Y. Crowell, 1968.
A good book for upper level readers, this book tells the story of how a butterfly undergoes metamorphosis and the changes that occur in the natural environment during the same time.

Goor, R., & Goor, N. *Insect Metamorphosis*. Atheneum, 1990.
Through real-life photographs, this book provides factual information on how insects progress through their life cycles and undergo metamorphosis.

Hawes, J. (1972). *My Daddy Longlegs*. Thomas Y. Crowell, 1972.
A Let's-Read-and-Find-Out book, the reader learns a great deal of information about daddy longlegs. The book tells a narrative story about how to catch and observe this creature.

Jeunesse, G. *The Egg*. Scholastic, 1989.
Describes the formation of a chick from the beginning within the egg.

Kalman, B. *Web Weavers and Other Spiders*. Crabtree Publishing, 1997.
The book describes spiders, their physical characteristics, web building, mating behavior, and survival skills. Vocabulary words are in bold print and the book includes real pictures of various spiders and webs.

Lane, M. *The Spider*. The Dial Press, 1982.
Through a narrative story and illustrations, the book describes several species of spiders, including their physiology, behavior, and mating patterns.

McNulty, F. *The Lady and the Spider*. Harper Trophy Books, 1986.
A spider who was living in a head of lettuce in the garden is returned to the garden by a lady who finds him in her house after picking the head of lettuce.

Neidigh, S. *Creatures at My Feet*. Northland Publishing, 1993.
Through a rhyme sequence, this book describes creatures that can be found at ground level. It takes the reader through a variety of ecosystems such as the beach, forest, and water areas.

O'Callahan, J. *Herman and Marguerite*. Peachtree Publishers, 1996.
An earthworm and caterpillar become friends as they attempt to rejuvenate an orchard that has been neglected over the years. Through their individual jobs, the orchard becomes fruitful again.

O'Hagan, C. *It's Easy to Have a Snail Visit You*. Lothrop, Lee and Shepard, 1980.
The book describes how to care for a snail as a pet.

Overbeck, C. *Dragonflies*. Learner, 1971.
This factual book describes the incomplete metamorphosis that dragonflies and damselflies undergo within their life cycles.

Owen, J. *Usborne Mysteries and Marvels of Insect Life*. Usborne Publishing, 1989.
An encyclopedia-type reference book, this book offers a large amount of factual information on insects. Colorful realistic illustrations offer detailed information as well.

Perrot, A. S. *Earthworm*. Creative Editions, 1993.
Describes the physical characteristics, habits, and importance of earthworms in the environment.

Perrot, A. S. *Egg*. Creative Editions, 1993.
Describes the characteristics of blackbirds and their eggs. This book gives information on what the egg does. It does contain information on fertilization of the egg that might be too graphic for younger children.

Perrot, A. S. *Gnat*. Creative Editions, 1993.
This book describes the physical characteristics, life cycle, and usefulness of gnats.

Pope, J. *Seashores*. Troll Associates, 1990.
Describes the characteristics of animals and invertebrates that live near the seashore. It provides well-illustrated drawings of many different creatures with exoskeletons.

Rowan, J. P. *Ladybugs*. Rourke, 1993.
The physical characteristics, habits, and behavior of ladybugs are described in this easy reader book.

Ryder, J. *Where Butterflies Grow*. Lodestar, 1989.
This beautifully illustrated book describes the changing from a caterpillar to a butterfly. It also provides the reader with gardening tips about plants that will attract butterflies to your yard.

Ryder, J. *When the Woods Hum*. Morrow, 1991.
A young girl finds herself surrounded by a humming noise in the woods when cicadas emerge from their dormant state. Seventeen years later she returns with her child as the cicadas emerge again.

Selsam, M. E. *Where Do They Go? Insects in Winter*. Four Winds Press, 1982.
This book describes where insects spend the winter. The book is broken down into chapters that provide information on the different types of insects.

Sammon, R. *Hide and Seek under the Sea*. Voyageur Press, 1994.
The reader is offered a great deal of information on various sea creatures from corals to algae to fish.

Selsam, M. E., & Goor, R. *Backyard Insects*. Four Winds Press, 1981.
Through realistic photographs and factual text, the book describes insects and their appearances, including camouflage, warning colors, and survival tactics.

Shepard, E. *No Bones*. MacMillan, 1988.
This encyclopedia-type book provides information on a variety of invertebrates along with a key to their identification. Pen and ink line drawings are provided to assist the reader in identifying the invertebrates.

Singer, M. *A Wasp Is Not a Bee*. Henry Holt, 1995.
An interesting book that compares creatures that are often mistaken for each other, there are several comparisons that fall into the category of invertebrates or insects.

West. T. *Zoe's Webs*. Scholastic, 1989.
One stormy night, Zoe finds herself on her own as she is blown from her mother's web. Zoe tries to spin her own web by imitating many designs she sees, such as those found on fences and hammocks. Finally, she learns to spin her own web.

Wood, J. *Coral Reefs*. Scholastic, 1991.
Provides information about coral reefs through a topic section and answer area. Vocabulary words are in bold print and an index is in the back.

Young, E. *I Wish I Were a Butterfly*. Harcourt, Brace, 1987.
A cricket wishes he were a butterfly as he encounters a variety of other insects. Finally, he happens upon a spider who helps him realize that he has special characteristics of his own.

Building an Animal Cell

Purpose:
- Identify the structures found in a typical animal cell by constructing a model.
- Explain how the structures modeled in the activity look similar to an actual animal cell.

Materials Needed:
package of gelatin dessert
banana slice
seedless grapes
fruit snack strips
maraschino cherries
resealable plastic bag
plastic knife

Introduction: For this activity, students will construct a model of a typical animal cell using gelatin dessert and fruit to represent a variety of subcellular structures. The structures include a cross section banana slice for the cell nucleus, the fruit snack strip for the endoplasmic reticulum, the grapes for the vacuoles, and cherries for mitochondria. (See page 66 for the diagram of animal cell.) All of these materials represent real structures that are found within the cytoplasm which is represented by the gelatin dessert. The materials used in this activity are edible, however, the medical history of the students should be checked first to insure that there is no allergy to any of the fruit or a blood sugar disorder like diabetes.

Procedure:
1. Prepare the gelatin dessert for use in the activity. Use half of the water required.
2. See student lab sheet for instructions.

Answer Key For Questions:
1. Answers will vary. For example, animal cells do not need to make their own food through photosynthesis.
2. Nucleus
3. It allows materials to reach all parts of the cell.
4. Answers will vary. For example, depending on the size of the cell, it may need to store or dispose of more food or wastes.

Literature Links: Jeunesse, G. *The Egg*. Scholastic, 1989.
Perrot, A. S. *Egg*. Creative Editions, 1993.

Portals for Expansion:
Language Arts
- Write a story about how the parts of a cell work together to form a living cell.
Mathematics
- Measure the size of an ostrich egg, one of the largest single cells known, and calculate how much bigger it is than a typical cell in the human body.
Art
- Illustrate other structures in our physical environment that can be thought of as existing as cells.
Science
- Explain the differences between plant and animal cells and why the differences might exist.

Name

Building an Animal Cell

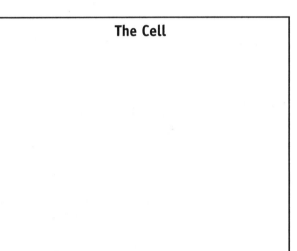

Procedure:
1. Using the plastic knife, peel several seedless grapes.
2. Cut a fruit snack treat into long strips about 1 cm wide and fold each back and forth.
3. Remove the stem from each maraschino cherry.
4. Cut a banana slice using a plastic knife.
5. Place a strip of the fruit snack in the bottom of the resealable plastic bag.
6. Fill the bag about one-third full with gelatin.
7. Place another strip of the fruit snack along one side of the bag, the banana slice in the middle, a grape near the other side of the bag, and a cherry beside the banana.
8. Fill the plastic bag about two-thirds full with the gelatin.
9. Put into the gelatin anything left over. Keep the items from "bunching together."
10. Seal the bag squeezing the air out of it, then refrigerate it overnight.
11. Draw a picture of the "cell" after it has become firm.

The Cell

Label the parts in your drawing:
a. The gelatin dessert is **cytoplasm** (the thick fluid in which the other structures are found).
b. The banana slice is the **nucleus** (control center of the cell).
c. The cherries are **mitochondria** (the powerhouses of the cell).
d. The grapes are **vacuoles** (storehouses of food or waste).
e. The fruit snack strips are **endoplasmic reticulum,** also called ER (a system of channels that separate the cell into different areas).
f. The plastic bag is the cell **membrane** (holds the cell contents together).

Questions:
1. Why do animal cells exist without chloroplasts which are found in plant cells?
2. What part of the cell is found singularly, that is, only one is found in each cell?
3. Why is the ER so long?
4. Why are there more than one vacuole in a cell?

Investigating a Pond

Purpose:
- Inspect living plants and animals, as well as non-living materials from a pond in order to do a biological survey.
- Measure the physical parameters of the pond including temperature and size.

Materials Needed:
pencils
string ball
magnifying glass
scoop nets
field guides

meter stick
thermometer
wash bottle
clear plastic tub (shoe box size)

Introduction: A pond is a good topic for study since it is large enough to house a variety of life-forms and yet small enough to be measured by conventional means. In this activity, students will be measuring the physical characteristics of the pond and looking for common macroinvertebrates. Using a field guide, living things can be identified. Encourage the students to use magnifying glasses to inspect the muds and algae collected and observe microscopic forms of life. It may be possible to classify the condition of the water on the basis of the kinds of life-forms that can be found in the pond.

Procedure: See student lab sheets for instructions.

Behind the Scenes: Safety is everything. Be sure to use personal flotation devices for any area deemed as hazardous. In addition, do a quick survey for other kinds of hazards including dangerous plants and animals that may be found around ponds in your region. Your local governmental wildlife services agency can be of assistance in planning for a trip to a suitable pond in a park and may have materials to assist you in the identification of life-forms unique to your area. In the United States, most states have an aquatic education specialist on staff who can guide you to a person in your immediate area. The agency may also be able to cite the licensing laws regarding the taking of macroinvertebrates from local waters.

Literature Links:
Cooney, H. *Underwater Animals*. Time Life, 1996.
Fichter, G.S. *Starfish, Seashells, and Crabs*. Western Publishing, 1993.
Neidigh, S. *Creatures at My Feet*. Northland Publishing, 1993.
O'Hagan, C. *It's Easy to Have a Snail Visit You*. Lothrop, Lee and Shepard, 1980.
Overbeck, C. *Dragonflies*. Learner, 1971.
Preller, J. *What's Bugging You?* Scholastic, 1996.
Selsam, M. E. *Where Do They Go? Insects in Winter*. Four Winds Press, 1982.
Shepard, E. *No Bones*. MacMillan, 1988.

Portals for Expansion:
Social Studies
- Write a letter to your local political leaders informing them of your findings while asking what it is that they do to protect the aquatic environment.
- Ask a representative from a governmental wildlife services office to speak on the importance of macroinvertebrates on the ecology of local ponds and streams.

Science
- Repeat this activity to investigate a stream. Compare the kinds of plants and animals living in this ecosystem with pond life.

Name

Investigating a Pond

Procedure: MEASURING THE AREA OF THE POND

How to Measure the Pond
To take a measurement, work with a partner and stretch a string across the selected part of the pond. When finished, measure the string length and record the measurement. Use a meter stick to measure the string as your partner rolls it back into a ball.

Identify the Shape of the Pond and Find the Area
Circular-Shaped Pond
1. Measure the diameter of the pond by stretching the string from one side to the other, going through the pond's center.
2. Divide the diameter by 2 to find the radius.
3. To find the area of the pond, multiply the radius times itself. Then multiply that times the value *pi* (mathematical constant with an approximate value of 3.14).

Data on Pond

Diameter: _____ meters

Radius: _____ meters

Area: _____ square meters

Rectangular-Shaped Pond
1. Measure the width of the pond by stretching the string from one side of the pond to the other.
2. Using the string, find the length of the pond.
3. Find the area of the pond by multiplying width times the length.

Data on Pond

Width: _____ meters

Length: _____ meters

Area: _____ square meters

Irregular-Shaped Pond
1. Using the string, take several width measurement of the pond.
2. When finished, add the widths and divide your answer by the number of measurements taken to find the average width.
3. Measure the length of the pond using the string.
4. Multiply the width times the length to find the area.

Data on Pond

Average Width: _____ meters

Average Length: _____ meters

Area: _____ square meters

MEASURING THE POND TEMPERATURE

1. Using a thermometer, take the temperature of the water in at least four places around a circular pond or on each side of a rectangular pond. Record the temperatures.
2. When finished, add the measurements together and then divide by the number of measurements taken to find the average temperature.

Temperature #1 = _____° C

Temperature #2 = _____° C

Temperature #3 = _____° C

Temperature #4 = _____° C

(total) _____ ÷ 4 = _____° C

IDENTIFYING POND RESIDENTS

1. Using the scoop net, scrape the bottom of the pond and bring up the mud, rock, algae, plant material, and animals collected in the net.
2. Quickly put the material into the plastic tub.
3. Use the wash bottle to squirt water onto the material washing it from the bottom of the rocks into the tub.
4. Carefully inspect the material in the tub for macroinvertebrates, or animals that you can see without the aid of a microscope.
5. Using a reference book, try to identify the specimens.
6. Using a magnifying lens, look at the plants and animals that you have collected. Draw them on the back of this page and label them appropriately.
7. Put some of the mud from the bottom of the pond under the hand lens and draw anything that you recognize as plant or animal material.

Questions: *Answer the questions on the back of the paper.*
1. How many indicators of good water did you find? How many indicating poor water?
2. Given the materials you were able to find in the pond, is the water in the pond in good or in poor health?

Building a Coral Reef

Purpose:
- Assemble models of individual coral to use in building a model of a coral colony.
- Identify the type of coral colony constructed from craft materials.

Materials Needed:

yarn or pipe cleaners	tape	scissors
colored paper	glue	craft materials

Introduction: Coral are individual animals that secrete a shell for protection. Most of their bodies reside within the shell with only the tentacles extending outward in order to filter the water and direct food into the organism. While there is no head visible, the tentacles direct the food to a centrally located mouth for digestion within the body of the animal. When the animal is at risk, it withdraws into the shell. As individual coral animals secrete their shells, they cement themselves to one another in one of several different geometric designs. Coral, generally, form six different shapes: mushroom, elk-horn, oculina, brain, rose, and organ pipe. Students will use small models of coral in order to build a shape that they will classify as one of these coral forms. While the organ pipe and mushroom are easiest to build, any of the coral shapes can be formed with enough care and patience.

Procedure: See student lab sheet for instructions.

Answer Key For Questions:
1. Answers will vary.
2. There will be a fair amount of variation among coral since they adapt to their environment.
3. The tentacles force the water into the coral so it can filter food out.
4. The shells offer protection from predators.
5. The tentacles can sting predators of the clown fish.

Behind the Scenes: Building one of the circular forms may require that the students wrap the coral with construction paper in more of an ice cream cone shape than a cylinder. This will make it easier to create a model of organ pipe coral. This time-consuming activity may be done as a project for several days.

Literature Links:
Boyle, D. *Coral Reef Hideaway*. Soundprints, 1995.
Cooney, H. *Underwater Animals*. Time Life, 1996.
Fichter, G. S. *Starfish, Seashells, and Crabs*. Western Publishing, 1993.
Sammon, R. *Hide and Seek Under the Sea*. Voyageur Press, 1994.
Wood, J. *Coral Reefs*. Scholastic, 1991.

Portals for Expansion:
Science • Research to find what elements are involved in building the shells which give colors to coral found in the sea.
Language Arts • Identify coral islands of the South Pacific, and write a report about the life that the people on the island have.
Mathematics • Measure the colony you make. Calculate, using a proportion, the size of the colony if a single organism is about 1 mm long.
Art • After reading the book *Coral Reefs,* draw a picture of a reef underwater and include other reef dwellers featured in the book.
Social Studies • Invite a marine biologist to discuss the value of the world's coral reefs with your class.

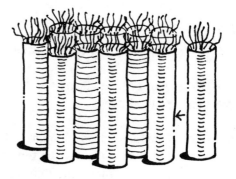

Building a Coral Reef

Procedure:
1. Work with a partner. Cut 25 cm of yarn from the supply or use pipe cleaners to make the coral.
2. If yarn is used, fold the yarn to double it, fold to redouble it, then double it one last time.
3. Wrap the folded yarn in a 3-cm square of colored construction paper.
4. Tape the colored paper loosely around the yarn.
5. Cut all of the exposed folds of yarn so that they appear to be tentacles sticking from one end of a shell or make the tentacles with pipe cleaners.
6. Repeat this process many times to have enough coral for assembling a colony.
7. Use glue to put the individual coral together. The "reef" is easier to build by using units made of one coral surrounded by six others.
8. Draw your creation in the space below.
9. Circle the kind of coral colony you have built from the choices shown below.

My Coral	Types of Coral
	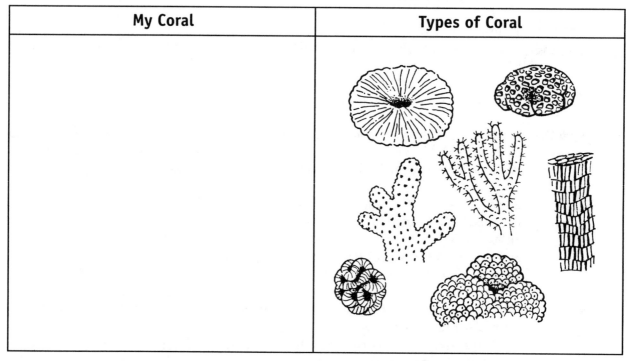

Questions: *Answer the questions on the back of the paper.*
1. How closely does your model resemble the picture of the same type of coral?
2. How much variation do you expect would be present within coral on the actual sea bottom?
3. How are the tentacles used by the coral animals in the colony?
4. How are the shells used by the coral animals in the colony?
5. How does a coral colony offer protection to the clown fish?

Test Tube Aquarium

Purpose:
- List the conditions that are needed to support life in a closed aquatic environment.
- Construct a balanced ecosystem within the confines of a test tube using living and nonliving materials supplied.

Materials Needed:

Collect from a lake or pond:
water
pebbles
mud
algae
duckweed
snail
sticks and other decaying material

Other science supplies:
test tube (16 x 150 mm or larger)
stopper for test tube
electrical tape or paraffin wax

Introduction: The components of the aquatic ecosystem include the nonliving substratum, water, and the biologic aspect, both plant and animal. In this activity, the students decide how much of each component is necessary for a successful aquatic environment. The students need to keep the discussion general, and then relate the discussion to the size of a test tube. To make the aquariums, each student must include enough algae to produce sufficient food and oxygen to keep the snail alive, while providing a limit to how much the snail can eat so that an algal bloom does not dominate the ecosystem. The students will come to appreciate the complexity of developing such a balance and will, no doubt, observe the results of nature creating the balance in their own ecosystems.

Procedure: See student lab sheet for instructions.

Literature Links: O'Hagan, C. *It's Easy to Have a Snail Visit You.* Lothrop, Lee and Shepard, 1980.
Sammon, R. *Hide and Seek Under the Sea.* Voyageur Press, 1994.

Portals for Expansion:

Social Studies
- Research the fringes of the Sahara Desert to learn how conditions have changed in this ecosystem, rendering it dramatically different than it appeared in the early 1900s.
- Contact the Exxon Corporation for a video that documents how the ecosystem around a major oil spill (Exxon *Valdez* accident) was cleaned.

Language Arts
- Write a poem about how the life of a snail in a test tube is like life outside the test tube.
- Write a letter to the appropriate governmental agency to find out how dangerous too much algae can become in a lake.

Mathematics
- Calculate the proportions by volume or by weight of the substratum, water, and living and dead organic matter used in the test tube.

LAB
Invertebrates

Test Tube Aquarium

Procedure: 1. Place your group name on a test tube.
2. Discuss how much of each material needs to be placed in the test tube:

Mud-

Sticks-

Water-

Algae-

Duckweed-

3. Add the amounts of material described above to the test tube.
4. Place a snail in your aquarium.
5. Make sure the contents will support a long lasting ecosystem.
6. Seal the test tube with the stopper. Secure the stopper with electrical tape or have your teacher use melted wax to finish the seal.
7. Keep the test tube in an area that receives indirect light.
8. Make daily observations of your aquarium and record the information on the chart.

	Date	Observations
Day 1		
Day 2		
Day 3		
Day 4		
Day 5		

The Case of Mistaken Identity

Purpose:
- Explain how the shapes of plastic six-pack holders, plastic bags, and other discarded plastic materials can harm animals in the aquatic environment.
- Identify which aquatic animals build a food web based on marine invertebrates like jellyfish.
- Evaluate personal actions regarding the disposal of various items of plastic garbage.

Materials Needed:
plastic garbage
large clear plastic container
water

Introduction: Items of plastic garbage are increasing in number and offer an increasing danger to the animals that may be part of a food web that involves creatures which the garbage may mimic. Plastic six-pack holders, plastic bags, plastic bottles and even plastic fishing line represent hazards for some marine animals. Some plastic garbage items, like plastic bags, appear to be jellyfish and plastic six-pack holders can become snares around the necks of fish and fowl alike. Discarded fishing line and plastic nets become dangerous traps for many species. What is the danger? What does the trash look like? What might try to eat the trash? What can each of us do to prevent the continued growth of this problem? Those are the objectives of this activity.

Procedure: 1. Collect plastic garbage from home or school. Clean it thoroughly and bring it to class.
2. See student lab sheet for instructions.

Behind the Scenes: Caution should be exercised when bringing in items of plastic garbage. Contents, such as bleach and food could represent health hazards due to the chemicals or spoilage that may be in the plastic. Therefore, clean the plastic thoroughly before allowing students to handle the plastic items.

Literature Links: Sammon, R. *Hide and Seek Under the Sea*. Voyageur Press, 1994.
Shepard, E. *No Bones*. MacMillan Publishing, 1988.
Wood, J. *Coral Reefs*. Scholastic, 1991.

Portals for Expansion:

Social Studies
- Write a letter to Cousteau Society, the Environmental Protection Agency (U.S.), or the National Wildlife Federation requesting information regarding the environmental impact of plastic garbage.
- Write a petition to establish, or support, a plastic recycling project at your school.

Science
- Draw a picture of a food web involving creatures for which your garbage may be mistaken.

Language Arts
- Write a report using the plastic garbage theme.

Art
- Create a poster warning of the dangers of plastic garbage by making a collage of items of plastic garbage used during the activity.

LAB
Invertebrates

The Case of Mistaken Identity

Procedure:

1. Look carefully at the plastic garbage that is laid out for you.
2. Identify each piece of garbage and record it on the data chart below.
3. Record how each piece was used on the data chart.
4. Identify something that can be an alternative for each item. Record it on the chart.
5. Fill a clear plastic container with water. Test each item in the water to see if it floats or sinks, then record your observations.
6. Describe how the garbage looks when it is in water. Be sure to view it from its side, top, and bottom.
7. Using a field guide, decide what animal the plastic garbage looks like.
8. Identify animals that may be placed in danger because of each piece of plastic garbage.

Name of Item	How Is It Used?	What Could Replace It?	Sink or Float?	Describe It	Looks Like . . .	Is a Danger to . . .

Life in the Soil

Purpose:
- Observe life that exists in the soil.
- Record the observations in a journal.

Materials Needed:
newspaper
small garden shovel
large bucket
magnifying glass
bug magnifier box
apron or old shirt
large resealable plastic bag
small piece of leather (from old shoe or purse)
water
soil

Setup: Collect the soil in large buckets without disturbing too much of the surrounding areas.

Procedure:
1. Provide each team of students with a few small shovelfuls of soil on a piece of newspaper.
2. See student lab sheet for further instructions.

Behind the Scenes: The best option for this activity is to take the students to a wooded area and allow them to kneel or lie down to observe the soil. Select an area that has rich soil where invertebrates are living. Good options include wooded areas where you can clear away leaves or carefully move decaying logs. It is important to collect the soil just before you need to use it so the soil does not dry out. For the second half of the activity, mold and mildew comes from the soil and piece of leather; plants sprout from seeds trapped in the soil; and, possibly, insects will hatch from eggs buried in the soil. It is suggested that students make observations on days one, two, four, five, seven, and eight.

Answer Key For Questions:
1. Answers will vary.
2. Answers will vary.
3. Answers will vary.
4. Answers will vary. For example, mold and mildew may have come from the soil or have been located on the leather; seeds could have been trapped in the soil; and insect eggs may be buried in the soil.

Literature Links:
Dorros, A. *Ant Cities*. Scholastic, 1987.
Edwards, P. D. *Some Smug Slug*. HarperCollins, 1996.
Fichter, G.S. *Bees, Wasps and Ants*. Western Publishing, 1993.
Hawes, J. *My Daddy Longlegs*. Thomas Y. Crowell, 1972.
Neidigh, S. *Creatures at My Feet*. Northland Publishing, 1993.
Owen, J. *Usborne Mysteries and Marvels of Insect Life*. Usborne Publishing, 1989.
Selsam, M. E., & Goor, R. *Backyard Insects*. Four Winds Press, 1981.
Shepard, E. *No Bones*. MacMillan, 1988.

Portals for Expansion:

Science
- Visit a greenhouse or have a local greenhouse owner speak to your class, describing how he/she avoids unwanted seeds and microbes in the soil.
- Place some soil on a petri dish with the nutrient agar (available from the high school science department) to observe soil nematodes tunneling through the agar.

Math
- Create a pie chart depicting the different things that are growing in your miniature environment. As a class, combine the information on a histogram to show the frequency of different life-forms found in the plastic bags.

Language Arts
- Write a short story about living in the soil from the viewpoint of one of the creatures you observed.

Social Studies
- Research third world countries to find out what difficulties the people may have in growing types of plants from seeds. Compare and contrast their types of soil to yours.

LAB
Invertebrates

Life in the Soil

Procedure:

1. Observe anything that is crawling around on top trying to bury itself back in the soil. Carefully place them in bug magnifier boxes and examine them. Make observations as your teacher asks for them.
2. Carefully push the soil sideways to spread it out evenly on newspaper. Make observations and record them on the back of this paper.
3. Pick up a handful of the soil and examine it closely using the magnifying glass.
4. Compare the results with other classmates.
5. Take 240 mL of new soil (not the soil you just examined) and pour it into the resealable plastic bag.
6. Place a small piece of used leather in the bag, then sprinkle the soil and leather with water.
7. Seal the plastic bag making sure to trap air in the upper part of the bag. Set the bag in a sunny location.
8. Check the bag on days 1, 2, 4, 5, 7, and 8. Watch for new plants or animals growing in the bag. Mold, mildew, seedlings, grasses, and small insects that were trapped in the soil may possibly emerge. Record your observations on the data sheet.

Questions: *Answer the questions on the back of the paper.*

Observing the soil:

1. What types of invertebrates do you see living in the soil?
2. Draw two of the invertebrates you observed. Include in the pictures details about environment and what the animals were doing.

Miniature environment:

3. Describe and draw pictures of the miniature environment each day.
4. From where do you think the new life came?

Life in the Soil Data Sheet

LAB
Invertebrates

Day 1	Day 2	Day 4
Day 5	Day 7	Day 8

An Earthworm's Heartbeat

Purpose:
- Identify the blood vessels in an earthworm and calculate its heart rate by participating in the activity.
- Explain that some "lower" forms of life have complex systems including organs.

Materials Needed:

clock or watch	water
flat pan	night crawler
paper towels	

Introduction: The night crawler is a large specimen of the common earthworm available from science supply houses, from live bait stores, or in rich soil. The earthworm is actually a fragile creature, for it breathes through its moist skin. Should the skin become too dry or too moist, the earthworm will suffocate or drown. It is important to keep the earthworms in the moist (not wet) medium in which they arrive (or in a moist mixture of half garden soil and half dry leaves or grass cuttings) until they are examined during the activity. The earthworm is a living creature and, therefore, must be handled with care. Be sure to touch the earthworm with wet hands and not squeeze or drop it. The earthworm feels cool because its body temperature is the same as the soil's. It may tickle the palm of your hand because of the short hair-like structures along its bottom side that help it move through the soil. The activity will center on a particular blood vessel that can be observed running along the top side of the earthworm.

Procedure: See the student lab sheet for instructions.

Behind the Scenes: The students can easily tell if the teacher is afraid of worms. It is essential that the teacher demonstrate proper respect for the life-form and for its care and use. If this is not possible, then another activity should be selected for use with the class.

Literature Links: Edwards, P. D. *Some Smug Slug*. HarperCollins, 1996.
Neidigh, S. *Creatures at My Feet*. Northland Publishing, 1993.
O'Callahan, J. *Herman and Marguerite*. Peachtree Publishers, 1996.
Perrot, A. S. *Earthworm*. Creative Editions, 1993.

Portals for Expansion:

Science
- Compare the heart rates of worms kept at normal room temperature with worms that have been refrigerated.

Social Studies
- Invite a farmer or agricultural expert to speak on the function that earthworms perform in preparing soils for use by farmers.

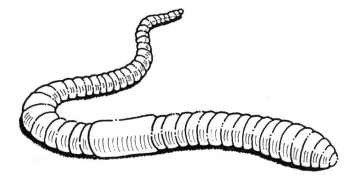

An Earthworm's Heartbeat

Procedure:

1. For this investigation, place several wet paper towels in the tray. The paper towels should be moist, not soaking wet.
2. Wet your hands before picking up the earthworm.
3. Carefully pick up a worm from the supply and place it gently on the tray. Respect this life-form. Do not squeeze or drop it.
4. Draw your earthworm in the box below.
5. Label the thick, smooth band that goes around the worm as the **clitellum.**
6. Identify and label the **front** of the worm by noting that the clitellum is closer to the front than to the back of the earthworm.
7. Allow the earthworm to calm down while it is on the tray. Should this present a problem, cover the head of the earthworm with a paper towel. Darkness will help to calm the worm.
8. Identify the **top side** of the worm, then label it in your drawing.
9. Identify the **bottom side** of the earthworm.
10. Identify and draw a dark line running along the top side of the earthworm. Observe it carefully.
11. The dark line is a **blood vessel.** Watch how it gets wider and thinner as the blood is pumped through the vessel by the heart. Draw and label the blood vessel.
12. Using a watch or clock with a second hand, watch the blood vessel for one minute and count how many times the blood vessel expands.
13. What is the heart rate for one minute? _____ beats per minute
14. Return the earthworm to its container and dispose of the towels. Using soap, wash both the tray and your hands.

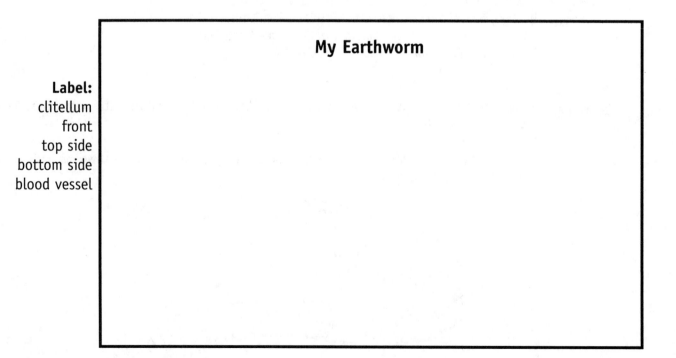

My Earthworm

Label:
clitellum
front
top side
bottom side
blood vessel

Create Your Own Insect

Purpose:
- Construct an insect model and name it based on its characteristics.
- Identify the main parts of an insect.
- Create an information page about the insect model and include it in the classroom field guide.

Materials Needed:
camera and film

For each student:

pipe cleaner	pony bead	scissors
small wiggly eyes	tagboard	pencil
hot glue gun and glue sticks	markers and craft materials	
flower stamens (available at craft store)	paper scraps	

Introduction: In this activity, students will have the opportunity to create their own insects using craft materials and scrap paper and compile information in a class book on insects.

Preparation: Using a paper cutter, cut the tagboard into squares for students to use when making the wings of the insects.

Procedure:
1. See student lab sheet for instructions.
2. Discuss with the students how the various adaptations found on the insects help them to survive.
3. Take pictures of the insects for the information sheets. Have each student describe his/her insect by noting its color, wing type, size, special adaptations, and life cycle, including its habitat, food, predators, and how it protects itself.
4. Assemble the information pages in a class book.

Literature Links:
Brown, R. *If at First You Do Not See.* Holt, Rinehart and Winston, 1982.
Facklam, M. *Creepy, Crawly Caterpillars.* Little, Brown and Company, 1996.
Fichter, G.S. *Bees, Wasps and Ants.* Western Publishing, 1993.
Overbeck, C. *Dragonflies.* Learner, 1971.
Owen, J. *Usborne Mysteries and Marvels of Insect Life.* Usborne Publishing, 1989.
Perrot, A. S. *Gnat.* Creative Editions, 1993.
Rowan, J. P. *Ladybugs.* Rourke, 1993.
Selsam, M. E., & Goor, R. *Backyard Insects.* Four Winds Press, 1981.
Young, E. *I Wish I Were a Butterfly.* Harcourt, Brace, 1987.

Portals for Expansion:
Science • Use scientific prefixes, suffixes, and root words to name each "insect" based on its characteristics.
• Create a habitat (diorama) for the "insect" and place it in a camouflaged location.
Social Studies • Invite a speaker who has travelled to the rain forest to speak on the variety of insects that are found there.
Math • Create a bar graph based on the length of the insect models. Research the length of real insects and show the findings on a graph.
Language Arts • Create and illustrate a story about your insect.
• Observe an insect preserved in amber and speculate on what it was doing.

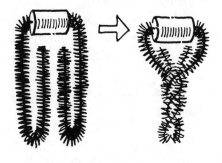

LAB
Invertebrates

Create Your Own Insect

Procedure:
1. Create an insect using the materials provided.
2. Bend the pipe cleaner in half and slide the pony bead to the center of the pipe cleaner. Bend each end toward the pony bead so the insect is one fourth the length of the pipe cleaner.
3. Holding onto the bead, twist the ends together to form the body. Pinch the ends to a point.
4. To make two wings, fold the tagboard in half. Draw a wing shape on one side of the tagboard, then cut out the shape from both pieces. Your wings will be symmetrical. Decorate the wings.
5. Glue the wiggly eyes and antennae on the insect's head. To do this, glue the eyes to each side of the pony bead. Bend the flower stamens in half (for the antennae) and glue them to the back of the head. Glue the legs and wings on the insect's thorax.
6. Complete the following information sheet about your insect.

- -

Glue picture here.

Name of Insect: _____

Physical Characteristics:

Insect's Habitat and Daily Life:

Composting with Worms

Purpose: • Build a composting container using two 2-liter bottles.
• Observe the actions of worms in the compost pile.

Materials Needed: two 2-liter bottles (one whole bottle with no base and the base from a second bottle)
black electrical tape
large piece of black construction paper
8-10 worms
worm bedding (shredded newspapers, peat moss, leaves, straw, soil)
scissors
permanent marker
nails various sizes
garbage (vegetables scraps, lettuce, bread, etc.)
aluminum pan
Exacto knife (for teacher use only)

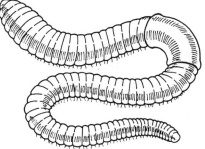

Introduction: Worms play an important role in the environment. These invertebrates do more than just serve as fishing bait. They aerate the soil, reduce the amount of organic wastes, and aid in natural decomposition and recycling. Worm composting has gained some attention during the past decade. Many people actually have large composting piles in their backyards since the compost makes great fertilizer. This activity offers the students an opportunity to examine a miniature version of a compost pile.

Procedure: See the student lab sheet of instructions.

Behind the Scenes: Red worms or fish worms work best in this activity. Avoid using nightcrawlers. You will need to keep the bedding moist but not flooded. Check the bedding once a day for moisture.

Answer Key For Questions:
1. Answers will vary.
2. The earthworms aerate the soil.
3. The earthworms may die because their skin needs to stay moist. If the worms were left in direct sunlight all day they would die and shrivel up.
4. Answers will vary.

Literature Links:
Edwards, P. D. *Some Smug Slug*. HarperCollins, 1996.
Neidigh, S. *Creatures at My Feet*. Northland Publishing, 1993.
O'Callahan, J. *Herman and Marguerite*. Peachtree Publishers, 1996.
Perrot, A. S. *Earthworm*. Creative Editions, 1993.

Portals for Expansion:

Science
• Gather information on the rates of decomposition for landfill materials. Prepare a debate for and against sanitary landfills versus incineration of garbage.

Language Arts
• Write letters to local landfills and garbage dumps requesting information about the procedures used at their sites.

Math
• Supply a bag of trash for the students to examine. Have them prepare a pie graph to show the amount of glass, paper, plastic, aluminum, tin, steel, and garbage contained in the bag.
• Create a line graph showing the rates of decomposition of a variety of materials in a landfill.

Art
• Prepare a poster, incorporating materials usually sent to a landfill, to communicate how long it takes for specific items to decompose in a landfill and/or naturally in the soil.

Social Studies
• Conduct a "town meeting" in the classroom to discuss the possible location of a "new" landfill.

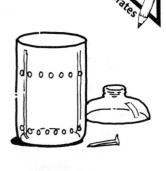

Composting with Worms

Procedure:

1. Cut the top off the first bottle approximately 2 cm above the shoulder.

2. For drainage, make a circle of holes by pushing a large nail through the plastic approximately 3 cm up from the bottom of the bottle. Repeat this step for air holes about halfway up the bottle. Set the bottle on an aluminum pan to catch the drainage.

3. Cut off the base from the second bottle. This will serve as a lid for the column.

4. To give the worms a dark environment, cut a piece of black paper that is wide enough to cover the entire column and yet extends about 5 cm above it.

5. Tape the paper sleeve loosely around the bottle so that you can remove it easily for viewing the worms and compost.

6. Prepare the bedding by shredding 10–15 sheets of newspaper into thin strips. (This will give you enough bedding for four homes.) If possible, use a paper shredder to make the bedding. Toss the bedding so the strips are loosely separated. The newspaper should not be clumped together.

7. Moisten the bedding in a large bucket of water by adding 480–720 mL (2–3 cups) of water. This is important because worms breathe through their skin and their skin must be kept moist. After the paper is saturated, remove any excess water by squeezing the newspaper. Retoss the bedding.

8. Mix in a few spoonfuls of soil into the bedding. This helps break down the bedding by using naturally occurring microorganism.

9. Fill the bottle approximately two-thirds full with the moistened, fluffed newspaper.

10. Place the worms on top of the bedding. Do not bury them, they will find their own way into the bedding.

11. Add small amounts of garbage such as vegetable scraps or bread. Add more every few days thereafter.

12. Observe your compost bottle on days 1, 4 (add garbage), 5, and 8. On the back of this paper, draw a picture each day to show what you observe and the location of the worms.

Questions: *Answer the questions on the back of this paper.*

1. What observations have you made about the worms?

2. Worms live in most soil types. How do you think they help the environment?

3. What do you think would happen to the worms if the soil was not moist? What would happen if they were exposed to the sun all day long?

4. What did you learn about composting with worms?

Invert Inventory

Purpose:
- Conduct a plot survey of invertebrates on a hula hoop sized section of the school yard.
- Identify, using a key, a variety of invertebrates that live in, on, and over the school yard.

Materials Needed:
hula hoops
magnifying glass
binoculars (optional)
invertebrates identification key
small shovel

Introduction:
While surveying a designated area of ground, students will identify a number of invertebrates which they do not usually notice. It is recommended that the selected area be part of the school grounds to limit safety and liability issues. Keep in mind that many terrestrial invertebrates have stingers, can cause allergic reactions, or carry disease. Students should be warned not to pick up bees. Depending on the area, encourage the students to wear long pants, long sleeve shirts, and caps to reduce the chance of picking up ticks and chiggers.

Procedure:
See the student lab sheet for instructions.

Literature Links:
Brown, R. *If at First You Do Not See*. Holt, Rinehart and Winston, 1982.
Facklam, M. *Creepy, Crawly Caterpillars*. Little, Brown and Company, 1996.
Fichter, G.S. *Bees, Wasps and Ants*. Western Publishing, 1993.
Hawes, J. *My Daddy Longlegs*. Thomas Y. Crowell, 1972.
Kalman, B. *Web Weavers and Other Spiders*. Crabtree Publishing, 1997.
Neidigh, S. *Creatures at My Feet*. Northland Publishing, 1993.
Overbeck, C. *Dragonflies*. Learner, 1971.
Owen, J. *Usborne Mysteries and Marvels of Insect Life*. Usborne Publishing, 1989.
Perrot, A. S. *Gnat*. Creative Editions, 1993.
Rowan, J. P. *Ladybugs*. Rourke, 1993.
Selsam, M. E., & Goor, R. *Backyard Insects*. Four Winds Press, 1981.
Young, E. *I Wish I Were a Butterfly*. Harcourt, Brace, 1987.

Portals for Expansion:

Mathematics
- As a class, create a histogram to show the number and frequency of invertebrate types found by the student groups.
- Estimate the number of invertebrates found in an area twice the size of the hula hoop, or an area as large as the entire school lot.

Social Studies
- Invite a scientist to discuss how invertebrates are used by this, and other, societies.

Language Arts
- Research the insects you observed in order to make a judgment as to the health of the plot of ground you surveyed.
- Write a field guide description of the surroundings in which the insects live including as much detail as possible.

Art
- Create a diorama representing your research area.

LAB
Invertebrates

Invert Inventory

Procedure: 1. Select an area of ground you would like to study.

2. Toss the hula hoop on the ground.

3. Carefully observe your choose research site.

4. Describe, in general terms, the area inside the hula hoop. Is it grassy or dirt? Is it wet or dry? Is it sunny or shaded? Is it isolated or heavily used?

5. Watch for any invertebrates, and draw them on the data sheet as you find them.

6. Turn over some of the ground by digging with the gardener's shovel. Draw the invertebrates you observe.

7. Watch the air space above the hula hoop. Draw the invertebrates you observe.

8. Use the invertebrates field guide to label the drawings.

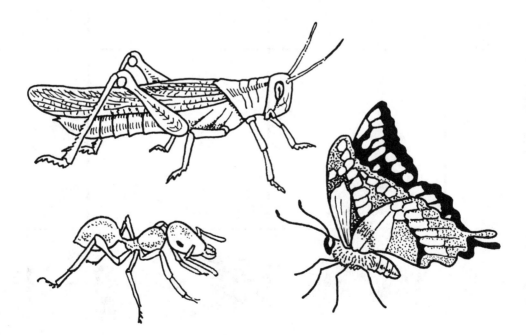

105

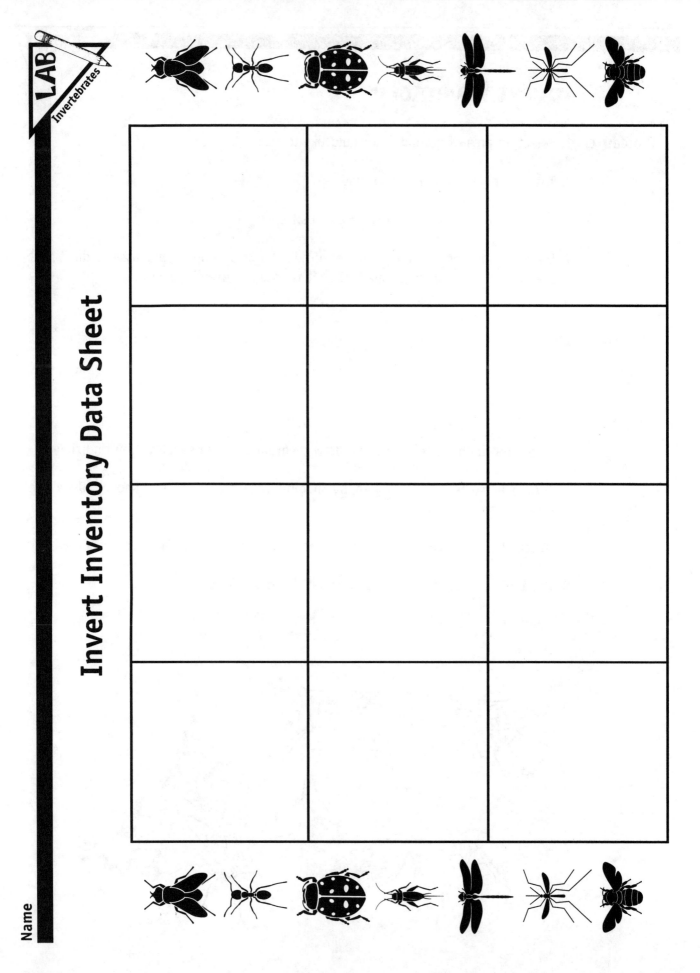

Name

Invert Inventory Data Sheet

Observing the Life Cycle of a Butterfly

Purpose:
- Make observations as butterflies progress through their life cycles.
- Record observations by drawing pictures that represent the stages of the life cycle.

Materials Needed:

For the class
butterfly house
butterfly eggs
food for caterpillars/butterflies
pictures of the stages of the butterfly life cycle

Per student
journal materials
markers and pencil

Introduction: The caterpillar hatches from an egg as a tiny larva, feeds and grows until it is time to form the chrysalis, then finally emerges as a butterfly. This is called a complete metamorphosis. In this activity student will make daily observations of caterpillars to assist them in explaining the life cycle of a butterfly.

Procedure:
1. Prepare the students for the activity by sharing the book *Charlie the Caterpillar* (if appropriate) to discuss metamorphosis.
2. Unveil the butterfly classroom area and explain to the students that butterfly eggs have been placed in the net.
3. Encourage the students to observe the area each day and record their observations on the data sheets. If interested, have the students create journals.
4. Carefully monitor the climate and food supply for the insects.

Behind the Scenes: Butterfly eggs and a butterfly house can be ordered from a science supply catalogue. Special instructions are included with the order. It is important to complete the activity at the proper time of the year so the butterflies can be released out-of-doors.

Literature Links:
DeLuise, D. *Charlie the Caterpillar*. Aladdin, 1990.
Facklam, M. *Creepy, Crawly Caterpillars*. Little, Brown and Company, 1996.
George, J. C. *The Moon of the Monarch Butterflies*. Thomas Y. Crowell, 1968.
Owen, J. *Usborne Mysteries and Marvels of Insect Life*. Usborne Publishing, 1989.

Portals for Expansion:
Science
- Encourage the students to explore other insects' life cycles to find out about incomplete metamorphosis and complete metamorphosis. Have the students share their findings with the class.
- Raise crickets and mealworms in the classroom to observe their life cycles.

Observing the Life Cycle of a Butterfly Data Sheet

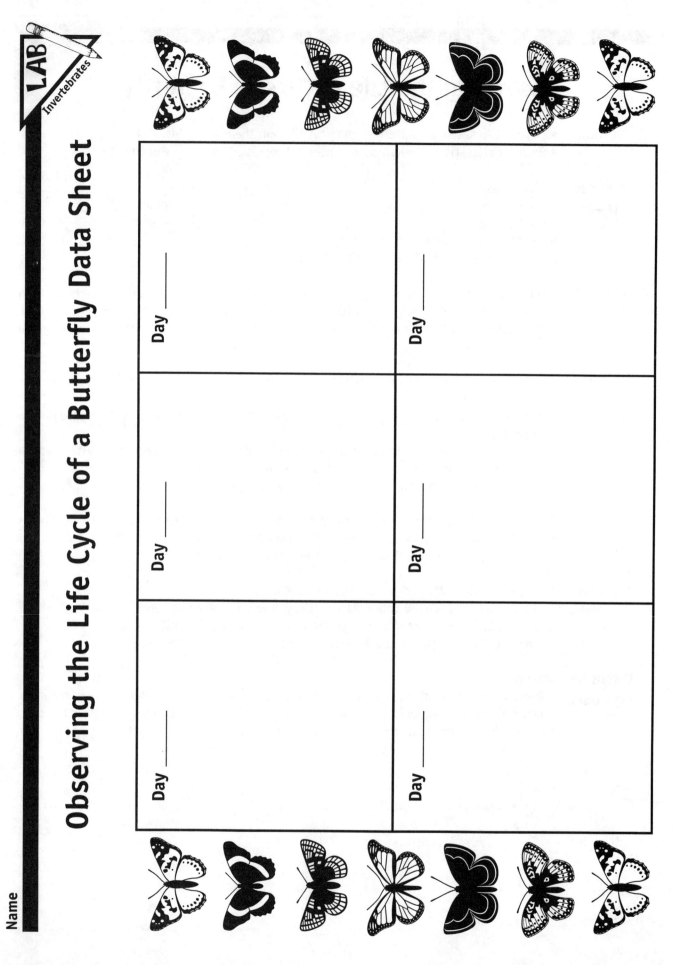

Day ____	Day ____	Day ____
Day ____	Day ____	Day ____

VERTEBRATES

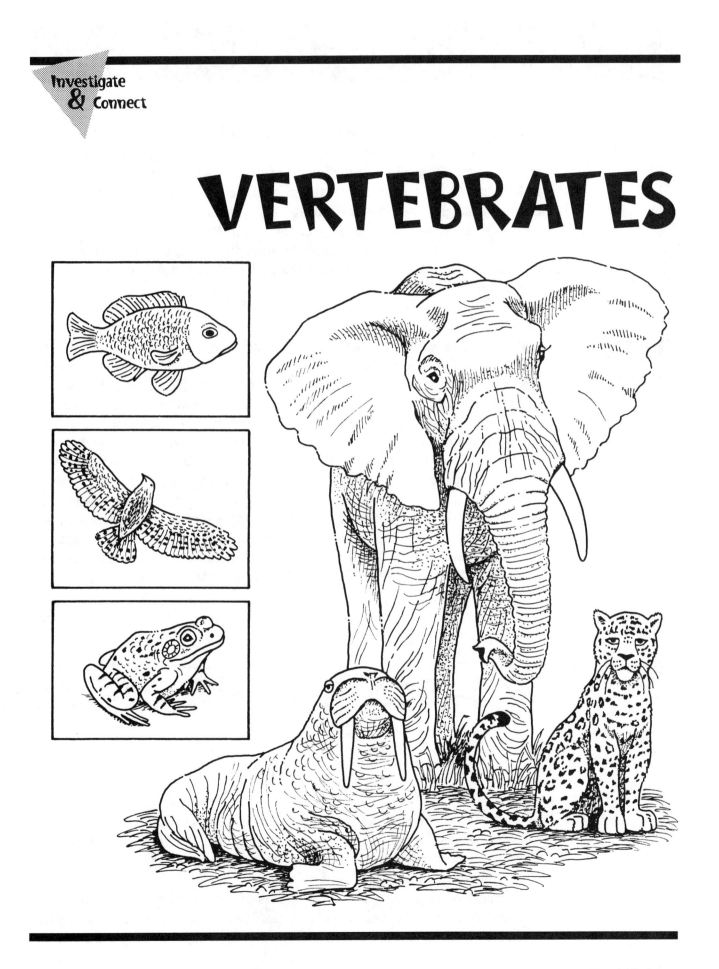

Fascinating Facts for Teachers

Vertebrates

Phylum Chordata, in which the subphylum Vertebrata is found, contains many well-known creatures that roam the earth. The common characteristic of all of these creatures includes the presence of a dorsal structure containing the main nerves that travel down the length of the animal. In most cases, the nerve is surrounded by a protective sequence of vertebrae that develops in the embryonic stages. Vertebrates are bilaterally symmetrical; their bodies look like mirror images to the left and right of the vertebrate column. More information about the different kinds of vertebrates—the fishes, reptiles and amphibians, birds, and mammals—follows. The human animal is more closely examined in the last section of this book.

The Fishes

There are three main classes to be examined in this section on fishes: the Agnatha (jawless fishes), the Chondrichthyes (cartilaginous fishes), and the Osteichthyes (bony fishes). The first group is the jawless fishes; the cyclostomes, with many species, have long, slender bodies and round sucking mouths. The name of the order Cyclostoma describes them: *cyclo-* for round and *-stoma* for mouth. Within the cyclostome's body are a two-chambered heart, a complete nervous system along with a well-developed brain, and other organ systems. The lamprey is a member of this order. It is a long, cylindrical animal which spends most of its time attached to and riding along in a parasitic relationship with larger fishes in both fresh- and saltwater. Some species are not parasitic, but the hagfish, for example, is still quite damaging as it feeds on fishes caught on commercial lines or netting. Attempts to control the infiltration of these creatures into the freshwater habitats of the Great Lakes have seen limited success.

Hagfish

The class Chondrichthyes are known as the cartilaginous fishes. The name describes the class in that *chondri-* means cartilage and *-ichthyes* means fish. They all have complete columns of vertebrae, moveable jaws, and paired appendages. They represent a very old group of animals with some fossil evidence of sharks reaching back to the large and thriving seas of the Devonian Period. This class includes the sharks, the rays, and chimaeras. They range in size from the dogfish (about 1 meter in length) to the giant, 15-meter (49-feet) long whale shark, which is a shark, not a whale (classified as a mammal). The skeletons of these fish are entirely made of cartilage with only occasional limy deposits that serve a reinforcing function.

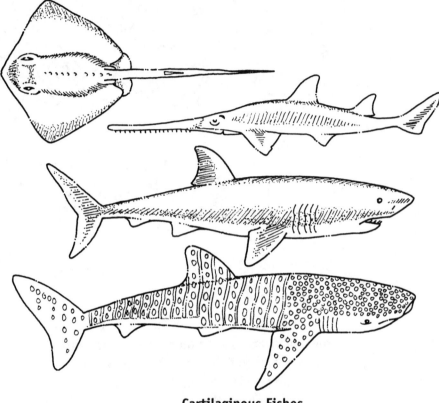

Cartilaginous Fishes

The shark is a much feared and misunderstood animal. Only several species will attack humans on purpose. The majority of shark attacks are due to the fact that a human swimming or playing in water is not very graceful and looks amazingly like a sick fish or seal. Many species of sharks have powerful jaws and can be a nuisance to fishermen as they tear through nets. Sharks are a common food for many parts of the world, but the popular beliefs among the U.S. population have limited the use of this creature for decades. Mako (shark) is now a feature in the best restaurants, and stamped shark is often sold as a substitute for scallops.

See Portal for Exploration "Make a Fish"

See Portal for Exploration "What Can You See"

The class Osteichthyes is also known as the "bony fishes." The major difference between these fishes and the cartilaginous fishes is that the skeleton of the "Osteichthyes" is largely ossified, or turned into hard bone. This class includes many well-known species: catfish, carp, trout, bass, sunfish, bluefish, and flounder. Osteichthyes live in saltwater, brackish water, and freshwater and range in size from a particular goby that is only 10 mm long to the Columbia River sturgeon that may be 4 meters (13 feet) long. The number of bones can be high by including both ribs and delicate intramuscular bones that extend between the ribs, as well as interspinal bones that help the movement of the dorsal and anal fin rays.

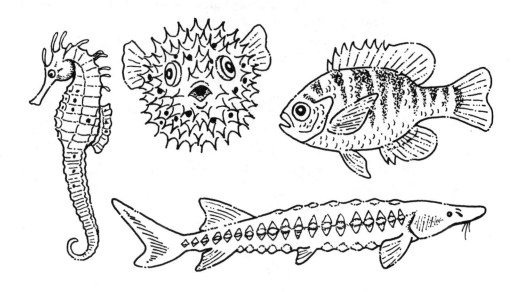

Bony Fishes

Most fishes are covered with scales that are small, thin, platelike bony structures. Some scales are uniquely adapted with spines (on the porcupine fishes) or are heavy and function as armor protection. In salmon and trout, as well as in many other species, the scales grow more from spring through fall, then a "winter line" is created by the startup of growth during the following spring. Counting winter lines is akin to counting the growth rings in trees and can be used to estimate the age of the scales. While some scales are lost and replaced, most of the scales will remain attached to the fish for its lifetime, preserving a record of growth rates.

Amphibians and Reptiles

The amphibians are creatures that start their lives as aquatic organisms and later transform into terrestrial animals. This class includes the frogs, toads, salamanders, and wormlike caecilians (that remain limbless throughout their lives as amphibians). Adult amphibians represent the lowest form of four-footed land vertebrates. Generally, an amphibian has moist skin, two pairs of appendages, nostrils with a kind of valve to exclude water, a bony skeleton, a three-chambered heart, a brain, and a variable body temperature. As the animal changes from an aquatic form to terrestrial life-form, the metamorphosis includes a change in the skin to permit exposure to air, modification of the body for terrestrial locomotion, development of limbs from fins, replacement (in many species) of gills by lungs with parallel changes in the respiratory system, and the emergence of senses that operate on land as well as in water.

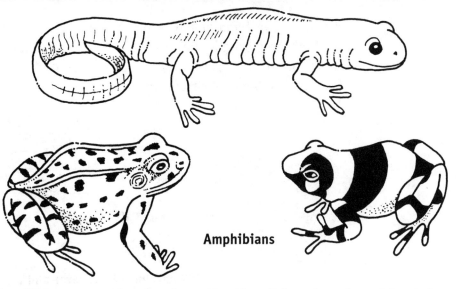

Amphibians

See Portal for Exploration "Raising Frogs"

See Portal for Exploration "How Does A Frog Catch Its Lunch?"

Amphibians range in size from the tiny Cuban tree frog (about 1 cm in length), to the giant Cameroon frog (up to 35 cm [14 in.] or more in length), then to a giant salamander (nearly 200 cm [6.5 feet] in length). Respiration in an amphibian can occur through gills, lungs, and even through a network of blood vessels in the mouth that are aerated under the mucus membrane there. Many species of frogs and toads have vocal cords that allow the animals to make calls. The calls of frogs and toads can be distinguished by the distinctive sounds. Adult amphibians eat only live insects, worms, and small molluscs. Large bullfrogs have been known to feed on small fish, birds, or mammals. Large amphibians have even been observed eating small individuals of the same species. The aquatic larvae of the amphibians have small mouths that enable them to only eat algae and small bits of dead and/or decaying organisms.

See Portal for Exploration "Redesigning Reptiles"

The reptiles include the turtles, crocodiles, alligators, snakes, and lizards. Each reptile has a distinct body, head, neck, tail, and short legs tipped by webbed feet and horny claws. The reptile's body is dry and scaly with legs suited for rapid locomotion. Its body temperature is variable, and it bears its young by laying eggs. Reptiles range in size from small lizards 5 cm (2 in.) or less in length to the regal python that may grow in excess of 10 meters (32 ft.). Large crocodiles are documented at over 7 meters (23 ft.) in length. Most North American species do not reach these lengths; most snakes are less than 2 meters (6.5 ft.) in length and most lizards are under 30 cm (12 in.).

It is easy to confuse crocodiles and alligators because, upon first inspection, their exterior appearances are very much the same. They can, however, be easily distinguished by the features that characterize the shape of their snouts. A crocodile has a snout that is more triangular and may be thought of as being more "pointed." The alligator's snout is more blunt. The differences between the animals are easy to spot if the animals appear next to one another, but if they are not, identifying which is pointed and which is blunt can be difficult. The teeth of the crocodile, however, also give a good identification clue. As opposed to its cousin the alligator, the crocodile's teeth of the lower jaw do not fit cleanly into its lips, being exposed even when the jaw is closed.

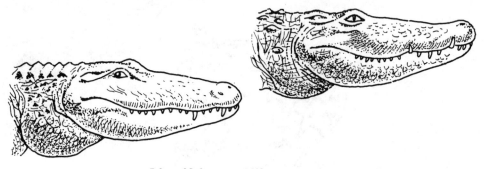

Identifying an Alligator and a Crocodile

Many reptiles are benefical to humans even though they are usually feared by people. Most snakes and lizards feed on rodents and insects, but some do feed on eggs of other animals, including domesticated and wild species. The image of reptiles as slimy, scary things is, in general, not deserved. Some snakes and other reptiles are poisonous, such as the two varieties of the coral snake (with black rings bordered by yellow), the moccasin, the copperhead, and about 20 types of rattlesnakes. Except for the coral snake, the poisonous snakes listed are pit vipers. The name "pit" refers to a thermosensor located between the nostril and eye on each side of the snake's head. The venom of rattlesnakes and other vipers affects the heart of the victim while the venom of the cobra affects the respiratory system. Antivenins are widely available for nearly every type of snakebite.

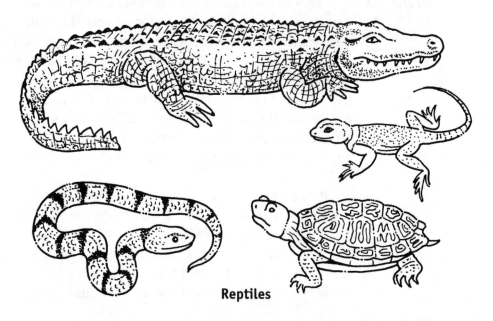

Reptiles

Fossil reptiles are another favorite science topic in elementary schools. Dinosaurs have been considered as extinct reptiles for decades. Examination of the pelvic girdle and related bony structures has caused a reconsideration of that judgment. In recent years, the theory that the dinosaurs are actually birds has gained popularity. Nevertheless, a review of dinosaur skeletons finds that they range in size from small, chicken-sized creatures to the giant species that have gained fame for their large sizes. Not all species of dinosaurs lived at the same time but dinosaurs, in general, were the dominant life-form for several periods of geologic history. Some of these massive creatures must have shaken the ground as they moved. What it was that caused their sudden death remains a mystery, but a cosmic collision with a meteorite or large comet is a theory being investigated with fervor.

Birds

The birds, class Aves in the phylum Chordata, are the most easily recognized class, due to the unique nature of the animals. A bird has unique characteristics which include a body covered with feathers and two pair of limbs, of which one is modified as wings for flight and the other for walking, swimming, or perching. Its feet are four-toed and are covered by tough skin referred to as "cornified." Its skeleton is very delicate with hollow bones that are uniquely designed to be lightweight for flight. The mouth has some kind of protruding beak or bill with no teeth. A bird also has a complete digestive system, a circulatory system with a four-chambered heart, respiration by lungs, and a complete nervous system. The sexes are separate and fertilization is internal. Eggs are laid to be incubated externally; later the young hatchlings are fed and cared for by the parents.

Birds

The size of birds varies greatly, with the hummingbird being among the smallest adults (7 cm [3.5 in.] in length), and the ostrich being among the largest (over 200 cm [6.5 ft.] tall). The ostrich egg, nearly 15 cm [6 in.] in diameter, is among the world's largest single cell. Yet, even at the size of the ostrich, birds cannot compare in size to the largest fishes or mammals. They are, however, an amazingly diverse group of animals that are the object of great popular admiration. Many people claim to be "birders," regularly searching their neighborhoods and keeping careful records of the birds that pass through their regions. Many bird-watchers will take trips to known bird sanctuaries in order to expand the number of bird species they have personally seen. These bird-watchers actually contribute significantly to the science of birds (ornithology) by documenting the presence and extent of the range of specific bird species.

See Portal for Exploration "Hatching Chickens"

See Portal for Exploration "The Shape of a Bird's Beak"

The description of a typical bird can easily be done through a discussion of the common chicken. It has a distinct head with large lateral eyes and a mouth that has an extended pointed beak. It has nostrils on the upper part of the beak. Ear openings are located slightly behind and below each large laterial eye. The head is attached to the body by a long, flexible neck. The body is covered with several types of feathers. The soft, under layer known as "down," is present on almost all birds at hatching, but present underneath the other feathers on only a few adult birds. Contour feathers provide the external covering and give shape to the bird. Some feathers are uniquely adapted for such purposes as covering the ear openings and providing strength so that the wings can give flight. Filoplumes are small, hairlike feathers found randomly throughout the plumage of a bird. Their function is not clear. Bristles are feathers with a short quill and a long shaft extending from the quill. They are seen on such birds as flycatchers and whip-poorwills. Feather color is given to the feather during its development and does not change except by wear and fading.

The skeleton of the bird is an important feature. The bones are often hollow with air spaces to conserve weight. The bird has a prominent clavicle (the "wish bone") to which the flight muscles are attached. It is the arrangement of the pelvis and keel that has recently drawn a great deal of attention. A similarity in that arrangement along with other skeletal features is why scientists now believe that some dinosaurs are related more closely to birds than reptiles.

The digestive system of some birds includes a crop where food may be stored and moistened. For these birds, this is the source of regurgitated food that is fed to the young. The stomach of the bird is where digestive juices act on the food, but an additional feature assists the bird in digesting harder and tougher materials. The gizzard is a muscular portion of the stomach in which grit, swallowed gravel or other hard material, acts on the food by grinding it into smaller pieces. This adaptation helps the bird since it has no teeth.

The variety in the class Aves is tremendous with some birds living on land, some in wetlands, urban areas, and rain forests; some building nests in trees and others in the ground; some species have domesticated forms, while many others are completely wild. Some birds are plentiful to the point of being a nuisance, and other species are endangered or close to extinction. While humans continue to appreciate many forms of birds for food, as pest control, and for pets, many forms have suffered from human activity. Habitat depletion and biomagnification of poisons are two threats to the survival of many species within this class.

Mammals

The mammals are referred to as the "highest form" in the animal kingdom. They include the familiar animals ranging from mice (at 4 cm [2 in.] or smaller in length) to the blue whale (exceeding 30 meters [98 ft.] in length). The mammal represents a relatively recent development in terms of the history of the earth with the first fossil evidence reaching back to the Mesozoic Era (time of the dinosaurs) with small rodent-like forms in the Triassic Period. Although mammals developed in the Mesozoic, they did not become the dominant life-forms until the age of dinosaurs ended, and the Cenozoic Era began approximately 64 million years ago. Their diversity and ability to adapt are the reasons mammals have dominated current geologic time.

The most commonly used animal to demonstrate the characteristics of the mammal is the domestic cat. Over its body, it has a thin skin covered with hair. The cat is given its form by a skeleton that has many of the same characteristic bones as the skeleton of the human. The teeth of the mammal are fixed in number and consist of only two sets unlike some "lower" forms that produce multiple sets throughout their lifetimes. The muscles are attached to the bones to provide movement, with some muscles in the face providing for a level of expression. This is no big news to the keepers of pet mammals who claim to recognize the expressions on the faces of their pets as expressions of their moods or comfort.

A four-chambered heart is typical of the mammals, and circulation uses a system of arteries and veins as the blood flows away from and then back to the heart, respectively. The cat shows the development of two carotid arteries and two jugular veins supplying blood to the head and the brain located there.

A complete respiratory system includes lungs, bronchial tubes, and vocal chords that gives a mammal its voice for communicating danger, pleasures, and companionship. Easily identified by its voice, the call of a cat for attention as its owner sleeps comfortably in a lounge chair is much different from the call used when caught in a potentially deadly situation. The ability to communicate in some species is the source of a great deal of investigation. Examples include the studies with dolphins and whales whose complicated vocal patterns may indicate an understandable language, that someday, may be translated into human terms.

Mammals

The variations within the class Mammalia are striking. Knowing that many mammals are marine while others are terrestrial is only the beginning. The whales, dolphins, and porpoises are fine examples of the marine mammals. A recent effort to preserve these species has resulted in the alteration of many fishing techniques previously used to gather tuna. The same nets that collected tuna often collected dolphins which were then sacrificed and canned with the tuna. New techniques and a higher level of concern regarding the issue has led many, but not all, tuna providers to exclude the mammals in their tuna products.

Mammals can vary in the size and shape of almost every physical characteristic. This includes the size and shape of the head, neck, body, legs, feet, toes, and tail. The giraffe has a long, thin neck while the badger has a short, thick neck. The long legs of the white-tailed deer result in the ability to produce the high speed necessary for running to safety, while the legs of the skunk do not need to be as long due to its unique defense mechanism. Some mammals can fly; bats prove that webbed fingers and a light body can produce enough lift for effective flight. Some mammals are pouched; marsupials (kangaroos, koalas, and opossums) carry their young outside their bodies for a varying degree of time needed for complete development. Mammals in the order Monotremata, such as the platypus of Australia, actually bear their young by laying eggs.

The primates represent the order in which the human animal is found. It also contains the lemurs, monkeys, apes, gorillas, and the chimpanzee. The care and concern for the lower primates (lower than the human animals) is only a recent development. It is now known that many primates have been hunted and threatened by the same kinds of human intrusions that have threatened many other kinds of animals. Using poisons for pest and herbicide control and the willingness to enter a habitat and alter it for other uses makes humans the greatest enemy of the lower primates.

Portals for Learning: Literature

Allen, J. *Whale*. Candlewick Press, 1992.
Anya and her mother witness what they call a "magical" rescue of a whale and her baby as the whales attempt to outrun an oil slick. This good book provides much information about how whales live and breathe.

Arnold, C. *Sea Turtles*. Scholastic, 1994.
This story tells about the journey that sea turtles take to lay their eggs, leaving them to hatch, and how they spend their lives in the sea.

Arnosky, J. *Watching Foxes*. Lothrop, Lee and Shepard, 1985.
Four foxes play in the sunlight near their den while their mother is away. This good book depicts pictures of wooded areas and habitats of foxes.

Arnosky, J. *Raccoons and Ripe Corn*. Lothrop, Lee and Shepard, 1987.
The raccoons raid a farmer's field of corn at night and quickly scurry home at sunrise. This interesting book shows the playful nature of these masked bandits.

Barrett, J. *Animals Should Definitely Not Wear Clothing*. Atheneum, 1970.
The book illustrates all of the problems associated with animals wearing clothes.

Barrett, J. *Animals Should Definitely Not Act Like People*. Atheneum, 1980.
A good book to use when discussing characteristics of animals, the book illustrates how silly and difficult it would be if animals acted like people.

Brett, J. *Annie and the Wild Animals*. Houghton Mifflin, 1985.
When Annie's cat runs away, she attempts to be friends with a series of animals found in the woods. Soon, she realizes that these animals are not suitable as house pets.

Buxton, J. H. *Baby Bears and How They Grow*. National Geographic Society, 1986.
This book provides the reader with information on several types of bears as they engage in different activities.

Cannon, J. *Stellaluna*. Harcourt Brace, 1993.
A young fruit bat falls into the nest of a bird and is raised as a baby bird. She encounters many problems throughout this experience and eventually finds out that she is a bat. Readers observe the characteristics of birds and bats.

Cole, J. *The Magic School Bus in the Time of the Dinosaurs*. Scholastic, 1994.
Ms. Frizzle takes her class on an amazing field trip back to the time of the dinosaurs. While on the field trip, her students learn a great deal about dinosaurs being related to reptiles and birds.

Cooney, H. *Underwater Animals*. Time Life, 1996.
A factual book, it provides vivid pictures and information about animals that live in a marine environment.

Craig, J. *Discovering Whales and Dolphins*. Troll Associates, 1990.
The book introduces readers to the characteristics and behaviors of whales and dolphins.

Crebbin, J. *Fly by Night*. Candlewick Press, 1993.
A young owl awaits the nightfall so that it can make its first flight with its mother.

Cunningham, A. *Usborne World Wildlife: Rainforest Wildlife*. Scholastic, 1993.
An encyclopedia-type book about wildlife, it provides the reader with information on amphibians, reptiles, birds, and mammals that live in the rain forest.

Demuth, P. B. *Cradles in the Trees: The Story of Bird Nests*. Macmillan, 1994.
This narrative book provides information about how birds build their nests and the materials they use in constructing them.

Dorros, A. *Rain Forest Secrets*. Scholastic, 1990.
Describes the layers of the rain forest and many of the plants and animals that live there.

Dorros, A. *Animal Tracks*. Scholastic, 1991.
The factual book describes animal tracks and other indications of animals. This book offers wonderful information when introducing tracks and signs.

Ezra, M. *The Sleepy Dormouse*. Crocodile Books, 1994.
This fictional story is about a weasel who traps a dormouse under a flower pot and feeds him seeds and nuts to fatten him up with the intent of eating him. The harvest mice free the small dormouse.

Ezra, M. *The Frightened Little Owl*. Crocodile Books, 1997.
In this fictional story, a little owl who is afraid to fly is tricked into flying by her mother who flies off and leaves the baby owl alone. The mother is actually watching the baby the entire time. Soon the baby owl is flying alongside of her mother.

Fichter, G. S. *Snakes and Lizards*. Western Publishing, 1993.
An encyclopedia-type book, the reader is provided with information on snakes and lizards, as well as good illustrations. Topics include specific types of snakes and lizards.

Fichter, G. S. *Turtles, Toads, and Frogs*. Western Publishing, 1993.
This encyclopedia-type book offers information on turtles, toads, and frogs. Good illustrations provide a great deal of information.

Florian, D. *Discovering Frogs*. Macmillan, 1986.
The book introduces the reader to a variety of species of frogs. Additionally, several pages are devoted to the development of frogs, from eggs into tadpoles into adult frogs.

Gans, R. *Bird Talk*. Thomas Y. Crowell, 1971.
This Let's-Read-And-Find-Out book tells about behavioral characteristics of birds, their nesting habits, and the foods they eat.

Gans, R. *When Birds Change Their Feathers*. Thomas Y. Crowell, 1980.
The book describes why and how different animals shed their feathers, hair, skin, and shells. Primary emphasis is given to birds.

George, W. T., & George, L. B. *Beaver at Long Pond*. Greenwillow, 1988.
This story tells about the many tasks the beaver performs during the nighttime, including building its dam and gathering food.

Grassy, J. *Eyes on Nature: Apes and Monkeys*. Kidsbooks, Inc, 1997.
A factual book, it provides the reader with information on apes and monkeys, including lesser known members of the family, such as lemurs. Photographs show monkeys and apes engaged in natural activities within their habitats.

Grover, W. *Dolphin Adventure: A True Story*. Greenwillow, 1990.
Through this narrative account, the reader learns about how a diver gains the trust and friendship of a dolphin family.

Hall, D. *Baby Animals: Five Stories of Endangered Species*. Candlewick Press, 1989.
An excellent book, it tells the story of five different animals species that are endangered. Through a narrative format, the book describes how these different animals interact with their own kind, find food, and survive in the wild.

Heller, R. *Animals Born Alive and Well*. Scholastic, 1982.
This book gives information about mammals, their scientific names, how they care for their young, and where they live. Factual information is presented in a story form.

Hirschi, R. *Who Lives in the Forest?* Dodd, Mead, 1987.
This easy-to-read book provides information on different types of animals that live in the forest.

Jenkins, S. *Biggest, Strongest, Fastest*. Scholastic, 1995.
An easy-to-read book, it tells about animals that fall into the category of biggest mammal such as the blue whale, the strongest animal, the fastest, etc.

Jeunesse, G. *Birds*. Scholastic, 1990.
Through this First Discovery book, the reader finds out about birds, their characteristics, and behaviors. This book has acetate pages that can be moved to show different pictures.

Jeunesse, G. *Frogs*. Scholastic, 1994.
A First Discovery book, it gives the reader information about frogs, their characteristics, and behaviors. The book has acetate pages that can be moved to show different pictures.

Khanduri, K. *Usborne World Wildlife: Polar Wildlife*. Scholastic, 1992.
An encyclopedia-type book with beautiful illustrations, the reader is provided with information on polar wildlife.

Kitchen, B. *Somewhere Today*. Candlewick Press, 1992.
This beautifully illustrated book describes characteristics of different animals "somewhere today" and provides an explanation as to their individual behaviors.

Kitchen, B. *And So They Build*. Candlewick Press, 1993.
Through text and illustrations, twelve different animals and their "houses" are described to the reader, providing information on the design and purpose of each structure.

Kuhn, D. *Turtle's Day*. Cobblehill Books, 1994.
Through actual photographs and a text that is easy to read, this book follows a small box turtle through her day, describing what she does.

Luenn, N. *Nessa's Fish*. Atheneum, 1990.
A young Eskimo girl combines creativity and bravery to save the fish she caught, which will feed her camp, from poachers.

Matero. R. *Eyes on Nature: Reptiles*. Kidsbooks, Inc, 1993.
An encyclopedia-type book, it offers information on reptiles, their behaviors, and habitats. The book contains actual photographs of different types of reptiles.

Matero, R. *Eyes on Nature: Lizards*. Kidsbooks, Inc., 1997.
This encyclopedia-type book provides information on lizards, their behaviors, types, and characteristics. It shows actual photographs of lizards in their natural environments.

Macer, A. *The Salamander Room*. Alfred P. Knopf, 1991.
A young boy finds a salamander and wants to keep it. His mother continually asks questions about its food and habitat. This helps the boy to realize that the best place for his salamander is in its natural environment.

Millen, C. M. *A Symphony for the Sheep*. Houghton Mifflin, 1996.
A good story to show that animals provide materials that people use, the book tells about wool being removed from a sheep by the shearer. The wool is then turned into wool thread and a final product.

Olson, D. *Eyes on Nature: Bears*. Kidsbooks, Inc., 1997.
This factual book provides beautiful photographs of bears and information about different types of bears.

Parker, N.W., & Wright, J. R. *Frogs, Toads, Lizards, and Salamanders*. Greenwillow Books, 1990.
Information is provided on the physical characteristics, habits, and natural environments of frogs, toads, lizards, and salamanders.

Powzyk, J. *Tracking Wild Chimpanzees*. Lothrop, Lee and Shepard, 1988.
Through the story, the author describes her visit to Kirba National Park where she observes and tracks chimpanzees. This book also describes the culture of the Burundi people.

Resnick, J. P. *Eyes on Nature: Cats.* Kidsbooks, Inc., 1994.
This factual book offers the reader beautiful photographs of various wild cats in their natural environments. It also gives information about the food and behavioral characteristics of these predators.

Resnick, J. P. *Eyes on Nature: Penguins.* Kidsbooks, Inc., 1997.
Beautiful photographs of penguins in their natural environment are provided in this factual book. It also describes the food and behavioral characteristics of these interesting birds.

Ryder, J. *Chipmunk Song.* Lodestar, 1987.
This book tells the story of how chipmunks spend their days in the late summer as they prepare for the winter months ahead. The book's format is almost a poem.

Selsam, M. E. *Egg to Chick.* Harper and Row, 1970.
An older book but the content is still correct, it explains how an egg's embryo develops into a chick. The book also provides pictures of the development at different stages.

Simon, N. *Benjy's Bird.* Albert Whitman & Company, 1965.
A young boy finds a baby bird and wants to keep him as a pet. When Benjy is convinced to let the bird go, he is surprised that the bird returns each evening.

Smucker, A. E. *Outside the Window.* Alfred A. Knopf, 1994.
Five curious baby birds observe what happens as a young boy gets ready for bed.

Sneeden, R. *What Is a Reptile?* Sierra Club, 1994.
This informational book provides a table of contents and index along with information on the types of reptiles, their physical characteristics, and their use of senses for their daily survival.

Weir, B., & Weir, W. *Panther Dream: A Story of the African Rainforest.* Hyperion, 1991.
A young boy is shown how to conserve life in the forest by a black panther. This book provides some information about animal life in the African rain forest.

Willis, N. C. *The Robins in Your Backyard.* Cucumber Island Storytellers, 1996.
Through a narrative story, the reader is provided with a variety of information about a pair of robins who build a nest, lay eggs, and care for their young.

Making a Fish

Purpose:
- Write a description of a fish and its habitat on an index card.
- Create a 3-D model of the fish using craft supplies.

Materials Needed:
construction paper
stapler
hole punch
craft materials (glitter, sequins, etc.)
newspaper
cardboard box/large shoe box
brass paper fasteners
index cards
bulletin board paper/butcher paper
glue
masking tape
scissors
yarn

Introduction: Not all fishes are alike. Fishes, like other vertebrates, have adapted to their environment in special ways. This relationship with the environment is noticeable when considering the fish's body shape, the kind of food it eats, its color patterns, and the way it reproduces. Students will study these characteristics carefully as they create models of fish and display them in dioramas.

Procedure:
1. Have each student choose a fish and find out where it lives, what it eats, how its body is shaped, and in what kind of environment it lives. When finished, the student records the information on an index card.
2. Provide a variety of craft materials and large sheets of paper for the construction of models. Encourage the students to form 3-D models of their selected fishes. One way is to cut out two side views of the fish from butcher paper and staple the pieces together along two edges. Stuff the model with small pieces of newspaper before stapling the remaining edges together to form the fish.
3. The model of the fish can be displayed in its habitat by creating a diorama. To make the diorama, cut out one or two sides from a box, then place the box so it opens to you.
4. Use craft materials to make the scenery for the diorama.
5. When finished, suspend or stand the fish in its habitat.

Literature Links: Cooney, H. *Underwater Animals*. Time Life Books, 1996.
Luenn, N. *Nessa's Fish*. Atheneum, 1990.

Portals for Expansion: **Social Studies** • Invite a local seafood restaurateur to discuss the various kinds of fish served and show where the fishes are found on a map of the world.
Mathematics • Compare the sizes of the actual fishes represented by models to develop a scale that details their relative sizes.
Science • Research different kinds of fish to find out about their special characteristics, such as an ability to change coloration.
Language Arts • Write a report on an aquatic habitat in your region and the fish population it supports.

What Can You See?

Purpose:
- Define the advantages of eye location on the side of the head or eye location on the front of the head.
- Apply the knowledge of eye location to define the niches of a variety of fish.

Materials Needed:
2 bathroom tissue cardboard tubes
elastic string
scissors
ruler

black felt
hole punch
paper and pencil

Introduction: All animals with eyes have adapted to life with their eyes placed in specific locations. Fishes that need to know precise directions and distances have eyes on the front of their heads for binocular vision. These fishes tend to be hunters, or predators. Fishes which are prey and must be ready to flee from danger tend to have eyes located on the sides of their heads. While these fishes lack binocular vision of predators, they have a greater field of vision and can see more angles for an early warning of the prospective attackers which may lurk nearby. Eye location is also important for other animals, including the world of mammals. For example, the eyes of a rabbit are set to the sides (greater field vision) but the fox has eyes on front of its head (binocular vision).

Procedure: See instructions on student lab sheet.

Answer Key For Questions:
1. Two tubes
2. Eyes forward
3. Side vision
4. The predators are northern pike, trout, and bass. The prey are carp, sunfish, and catfish.

Literature Links:
Cooney, H. *Underwater Animals.* Time Life Books, 1996.
Grover, W. *Dolphin Adventure: A True Story.* Greenwillow, 1990.
Luenn, N. *Nessa's Fish.* Atheneum, 1990.

Portals for Expansion:

Social Studies
- Explain why the human animal has both eyes on the front of the head.

Mathematics
- Measure the accuracy in touching the bull's eye and arrive at averages for trials with an eye patch and trials with two tubes.

Language Arts
- Read Boyle's *Coral Reef Hideaway*. Have students identify the variety of fish in the story and, based on the eye location, classify each as predator or prey.

Art
- Draw a picture of a fish and classify it as a predator or prey based on eye location.

Science
- Look at a picture of the flounder and speculate as to whether it is a predator or prey. Find pictures of other fish, those which live in coral reefs, open sea, or kelp forests, and determine if each is a predator or prey.

What Can You See?

Procedure: **Making an eye patch**

1. Cut out a 51 mm circle from black felt. Punch two holes in the felt. Thread a piece of elastic string through each hole, then tie the string to secure it to the patch.
2. Tie the ends of the string together to wear the patch over one eye.

Finding the target

1. Draw a bull's eye target on a piece of paper.
2. Hang the target on a wall.
3. Place a cardboard tube in front of one eye and the eye patch over the other eye.
4. Look at the target through the tube. At the same time, touch the bull's eye with a pencil. Draw a small "X."
5. Remove the eye patch and the tube.
6. Hold a tube in front of each eye with one hand. At the same time, try to touch the bull's eye with the pencil. Draw a small "X."
7. Compare your results.

Questions: *Answer questions 1–3 on the back of the paper.*

1. Which way is easier to touch the bull's eye?
2. Which arrangement is more like a predator that needs to judge distances accurately?
3. Which arrangement is more like prey that needs to see in different directions?
4. Study the eyes of the fish shown below. Circle the predators. Draw an "X" on each prey.

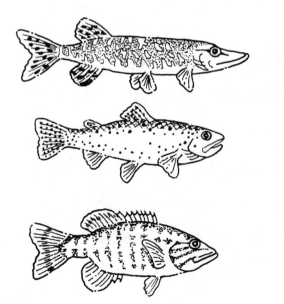

Raising Frogs

Purpose:
- Apply all principles in the care and respect for living creatures by raising frogs from eggs.
- Describe the frog's stages of growth from tadpole to its adult form.
- Explain metamorphism and how it is demonstrated by a frog.

Materials Needed:
aquarium
gravel
frog eggs (from science supplier)

algae
fish food
nonchlorinated water or pond water

Introduction: The frog is an amphibian that goes through a complete metamorphosis during its stages of growth. It is important to begin the activity soon after receiving the live materials from the supplier. First, prepare the aquarium by forming a 3 cm layer of gravel on the bottom. Add several centimeters of nonchlorinated water containing some algae and a good sized rock which breaches the surface. Instructions from the supplier will have detailed directions and should be followed. Adapt the general instructions below to the specific frog species that you acquire. Students should be encouraged, through a structured time, to record their observations by writing about and drawing pictures of what they see.

Procedure:
1. Place the eggs in a well balanced aquarium (room temperature water). Living eggs quickly turn black. If the egg mass turns white, discard it.
2. Watch for hatching within two days.
3. Tadpoles will eat fish food, but the algae in the water should supplement the feeding.
4. Have the students record how the tadpoles move and draw several pictures to explain this process in their journals.
5. Encourage the students to observe the beginning of the metamorphosis from tadpole into frog by watching for the development of legs.
6. Observe what happens to the tail as the tadpole continues to grow and change in shape.
7. If possible, release the adult frogs into the wild near a lake, pond, or in a wetland area.

Behind the Scenes: Materials needed for this activity are available from biological supply companies and require little attention. The students, however, will want to care for the tadpoles to a degree that exceeds the need. Frightening them by tapping on the glass, handling them in a rough manner, and nudging them with pencils are examples of improper behavior. The students need to treat the animals in the same manner that they themselves want to be treated.

Literature Links:
Fichter, G. S. *Turtles, Toads, and Frogs*. Western Publishing, 1993.
Florian, D. *Discovering Frogs*. Macmillan, 1986.
Jeunesse, G. *Frogs*. Scholastic, 1994.
Parker, N.W., & Wright, J. R. *Frogs, Toads, Lizards, and Salamanders*. Greenwillow, 1990.

Portals for Expansion:
Social Studies
- Find out why wetlands are important ecosystems.
Mathematics
- Compare the number of eggs and the number of actual hatchings using a ratio.
- Graph the growth, in terms of overall length, of the tadpole from its hatching to its adult-form.
Language Arts
- Write a journal regarding observations made during the development of the frog, and use it to write a story about the process.

Raising Frogs

Procedure: 1. Describe how the tadpole moves. Draw pictures to show how it happens.

2. Watch for tiny legs that start to form on the tadpole's body. This is the beginning of a metamorphosis. Write about and draw what you observe.

3. Watch for changes in the tail as the tadpole develops into a frog. Write about and draw what you observe.

How Does a Frog Catch Its Lunch?

Purpose:
- Describe how a frog, toad, or lizard uses its tongue to capture insects.
- Explain that animals have adaptations that assist them in survival.

Materials Needed:
party blower
3 cm strip of Velcro
30 cm piece of string or ribbon
pencil
graph paper

Introduction: Frogs are found throughout the world with the exception of Antarctica. They live in ponds, lakes, marshes, and other wetland areas. To capture insects, a frog uses its long sticky tongue which is attached to the front of its mouth. The frog flips its tongue over and out and then draws it back into its mouth after capturing the prey. This is an example of an adaptation that aids the frog in its survival. In this activity, each student has the opportunity to attempt to "capture" prey by using a simulated frog's tongue.

Procedure:
1. Find out what your students already know about how a frog, toad, or some lizards capture food. Using pictures, explain that some animals have special adaptations that enable them to catch their food.
2. See instructions on student lab sheet.

Answer Key For Questions: Answers will vary for questions 1–4.
5. Answers will vary. For example, the frog moves its long, sticky tongue quickly to catch insects.
6. Answers will vary.

Behind the Scenes: The longer the party blower the more difficult the challenge is to "catch" the fly. You may wish to purchase short party blowers for your students to use.

Literature Links: Fichter, G. S. *Turtles, Toads, and Frogs*. Western Publishing, 1993.
Florian, D. *Discovering Frogs*. Macmillan, 1986.
Jeunesse, G. *Frogs*. Scholastic, 1994.
Matero, R. *Eyes on Nature: Reptiles*. Kidsbooks, 1993.
Matero, R. *Eyes on Nature: Lizards*. Kidsbooks, 1997.
Parker, N.W., & Wright, J. R. *Frogs, Toads, Lizards, and Salamanders*. Greenwillow, 1990.

Portals for Expansion: **Science** • Collect pictures from nature magazines of frogs, toads, and lizards attempting to catch their prey. Compare the sizes of the tongues.
Mathematics • Using the information collected from the activity, have students determine if accuracy improves the longer they practice catching the insects.
• Make a chart that shows the different types of frogs in the world and their sizes.
Social Studies • Research the different regions of the world in which frogs are found. Give information on the type of frog and if it is important to each ecosytem or people's life style.
Language Arts • Write a descriptive story from the insect's perspective about how it feels to avoid being caught or from the frog's perspective about the frustration of attempting to catch insects.

How Does a Frog Catch Its Lunch?

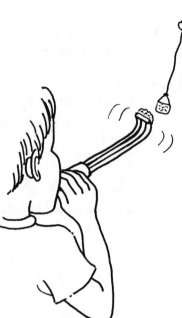

Procedure:

1. Unroll the party blower so that the end is in your hand.

2. Attach the "rough" piece of Velcro to the party blower by folding it over the end. (This is the frog's tongue.)

3. Make a loop with the string.

4. Attach the "soft" piece of Velcro to this loop by folding it over the end of the loop. This secures the Velcro on both sides of the string. (This is the "fly.")

5. Working with a partner, take turns pretending to be a "frog" and try to catch the "food" as your partner slowly dangles the string or "fly" in front of the party blower.

6. Predict how many flies you can catch in a minute. Record your estimate.

7. Have your partner count how many times you try to catch the fly in one minute and how many flies are actually caught. Make a graph to show the results.

8. Discuss the results. Are frogs and lizards better at catching insects than humans? Why?

Questions:

1. How many flies did you predict that you could catch in one minute?

2. How many flies did you actually catch in one minute?

3. How many times did you try to catch flies in a minute?

4. On the back of the paper, make a bar graph to show the number of flies you caught and the number of attempts you made.

5. Explain why a frog's tongue is a special adaptation that helps in its survival.

6. Describe how you felt trying to catch "flies" with your constructed frog's tongue.

Redesigning Reptiles

Purpose:
- Recognize the main parts of a reptile by creating a model.
- Construct a reptile and name it based on its characteristics.
- Create an information page about the reptile and include it in the classroom field guide.

Materials Needed:

For each student:

		For the class:
egg cartons	felt/fabric scraps	terrarium
bathroom tissue cardboard tube	clay or play dough	live reptile
tempera paints	1-liter soda bottle	camera and film
pipe cleaners	pony beads	food source
small wiggly eyes	tagboard	
hot glue gun and glue	watercolor markers	

Introduction: Reptiles come in various shapes and sizes, textures, and colors. Examples range from crocodiles to turtles to lizards. In this activity, students will have an opportunity to create their own reptiles using craft materials and scrap paper. A classroom field guide will also be compiled that will include a reference sheet for each reptile model. If interested, continue this activity by studying other animal groups. For example, students can create models of birds with craft materials. Before starting the activity, encourage the students to observe birds for several days and then construct the models and complete the field guide sheets for the class book.

Procedure:
1. Set up a classroom terrarium and place either a turtle or lizard in it.
2. Allow the reptile to be present for several days for the students to observe and record information about its behavior, habitat, food preferences, and its physical characteristics.
3. After five or more days, draw the students into a discussion about what characteristics help the reptile to survive, how it catches its food, and the habitat it prefers. Topics may include claws, coloration, mouth shape, protective devices, etc. List the characteristics on a chart.
4. Ask the students to brainstorm different ways reptiles have adapted to their habitats and record these on the chart. Have the students support their ideas.
5. Tell the students that they will have an opportunity to "redesign" reptiles by creating models, using what they know about these animals.
6. Provide the students with craft materials to use. Have each student sketch his or her ideas first before constructing the model.
7. When the students have redesigned their reptiles, have them explain the animals' adaptations to the class.
8. Have each student complete a "Animal Fact Sheet" for the class book on reptiles.
9. Include a picture of the student's reptile on the information page.

Behind the Scenes: If you choose to set up a classroom terrarium with a reptile, it is important to maintain the safety and show respect for the creature. Students should not overhandle the reptile. The conditions of its habitat and climate should be maintained consistently; it may be necessary to provide special care on the weekends.

Literature Links:

Arnold, C. *Sea Turtles*. Scholastic, 1994.
Fichter, G. S. *Snakes and Lizards*. Western Publishing, 1993.
Fichter, G. S. *Turtles, Toads, and Frogs*. Western Publishing, 1993.
Matero. R. *Eyes on Nature: Reptiles*. Kidsbooks, 1993.
Matero, R. *Eyes on Nature: Lizards*. Kidsbooks, 1997.
Parker, N.W., & Wright, J. R. *Frogs, Toads, Lizards, and Salamanders*. Greenwillow, 1990.
Sneeden, R. *What Is a Reptile?* Sierra Club, 1994.

Portals for Expansion:

Science
- Use scientific prefixes, suffixes, and root words to name the reptile models based on their characteristics.
- Find out about any reptiles which are endangered species.
- Create a habitat for the reptile model to show where it would live. Display the reptile in a camouflaged location within the diorama.
- Study other animal groups and construct models and complete fact sheets for class field guides.

Social Studies
- Discuss how some reptiles influence the economy in some regions of the world, such as the effects of the demand for alligator skin.

Mathematics
- Research the gestation periods for different reptiles and create a time line showing how long each one takes to hatch.

Language Arts
- Gather stories or folklore about different types of reptiles and start a classroom library.

Animal Fact Sheet

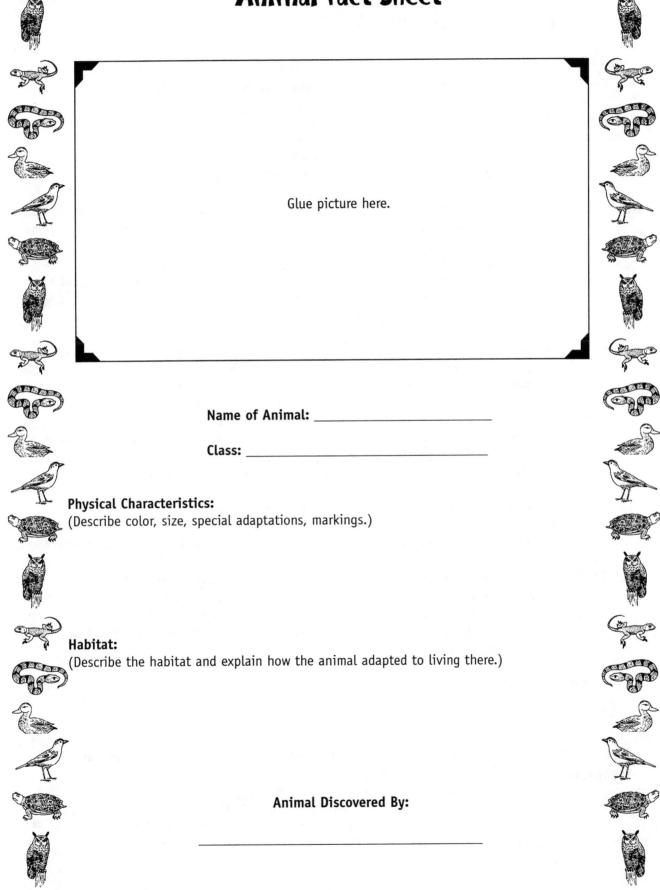

Glue picture here.

Name of Animal: _____

Class: _____

Physical Characteristics:
(Describe color, size, special adaptations, markings.)

Habitat:
(Describe the habitat and explain how the animal adapted to living there.)

Animal Discovered By:

_____

Hatching Chickens

Purpose:
- Identify the various parts of a developing egg by observing the activity.
- Record in a journal the changes that an egg undergoes as it develops.

Materials Needed:

incubator	water
fertilized eggs	sponge
china marker	pencil
bright flashlight	clear plastic dish or watch glass

Introduction: This long-term observation involves live animals. Proper respect for living things must be exercised and enforced. The students may need to be reminded that each part of the egg has a function. The yolk serves as the food, the albumen provides the water, the air sac provides a surface for diffusion of air, the membranes keep things separated, and the shell is protection for the outside environment. The incubator provides the required conditions for development, including warmth, humidity, and protection. The students need to rotate the eggs making sure that the warmth is evenly distributed.

Procedure:
1. Break an unfertilized egg into a watch glass and observe the various parts of the egg.
2. Draw an intact egg and label the yolk (yellow), albumen (white), air sac, membrane, and shell.
3. Wet a sponge and place it inside the incubator to provide humidity.
4. Carefully mark each egg with the date it was inserted into the incubator.
5. Turn on the incubator. Adjust the thermostat to about 100° F (68° C).
6. Using the date as a reference point, rotate each egg one third of the way around each day.
7. At about day 8, "candle" each egg by placing it in front of a flashlight in a dark room.
8. Look for eyespots, spinal cord, and/or heart. Draw what is observed.
9. Dispose of any egg that is cracked or infertile by day 10.
10. Candle each egg again at day 17 and draw what is observed.
11. Dispose of any egg with dead embryo by day 19.
12. At about day 21, the eggs will hatch. Some chicks will require help emerging from the shells.

Behind the Scenes: Fertilized chicken eggs are generally available from farm supply stores or, more rarely, pet stores. In the United States, it is very common for "county extension services" or "agricultural agents" to have incubators for loan at low or no charge. A call to the appropriate agricultural service may yield information on the availability of an incubator. New hatchlings can be sold to farm stores or pet shops.

Literature Links:
Gans, R. *Bird Talk*. Thomas Y. Crowell, 1971.
Jeunesse, G. *Birds*. Scholastic, 1990.
Selsam, M. E. *Egg to Chick*. Harper and Row, 1970.

Portals for Expansion:
Science • Compare the embryos of chicks to embryos of other animals such as reptiles or oviparous (egg-laying) mammals.
Mathematics • Track the size of the embryo and graph its development.
• Compare the incubation period of other birds to that of the chicks using percentages.
Language Arts • Write a creative comparison of the conditions provided by the incubator to the conditions provided by the mother in nature.

Hatching Chickens

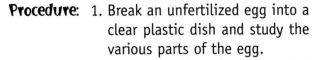

Procedure:

1. Break an unfertilized egg into a clear plastic dish and study the various parts of the egg.

2. Draw an intact egg and label the following parts:
   - the yolk (yellow)
   - albumen (white)
   - air sac
   - membrane
   - shell

3. Carefully mark the egg with the date it is inserted into the incubator.

4. Using the date as a reference point, rotate the egg one third of the way around each day.

5. On day 8, "candle" each egg by placing it in front of a flashlight in a dark room. Look for eye-spots, spinal cord, and/or heart. Draw what is observed.

6. Candle each egg again on day 17 and draw what is observed.

7. Sometime around day 21, the eggs will hatch. Some chicks will require help emerging from their shells.

The Shape of a Bird's Beak

Purpose:
- Describe the different shapes of bird beaks.
- Explain how the shape of a bird's beak helps the bird obtain the food it eats.
- Explain how birds' beaks are special adaptations.

Materials Needed:
pliers or tweezers
straws
coffee stirrers
kitchen spoons
clothespins
egg carton
beads
soda bottle
cotton balls
small plastic fish
pictures of various birds
shallow pan

Introduction: The shape of a bird's beak serves a very important purpose in its survival. Different birds have differently shaped beaks. The hummingbird has a very thin beak resembling a straw which allows it to sip the nectar from a bell-shaped flower; the cardinal's triangular-shaped beak is used to break open the shells of various seeds; and the pelican's large scoop-shaped beak allows it to catch fish. In this activity, students will have the opportunity to experiment with different "beak shapes" to find out how this adaptation helps each bird to survive.

Procedure:
1. Show the class pictures of a few birds with differently shaped beaks.
2. Ask the students to make observations about the shape of each beak, the type of bird pictured, and the kind of food it eats.
3. Explain that birds have beaks in certain shapes to assist them in obtaining food. The shape of the beak is a special adaptation.
4. Place the following items into a shallow pan:
   - beads to represent seeds such as sunflowers
   - cotton balls to represent different types of berries
   - small plastic fish to represent aquatic life forms
   - the egg carton with beads in it to represent a tree with insects
   - a soda bottle to represent the opening of a flower
5. Ask the students to find out which type of beak is best suited for obtaining certain foods.
6. See the student lab sheet for further instructions.
7. Discuss the results of the activity.

Behind the Scenes: This activity may be done as a demonstration or offered in a learning center depending on the size of the class. Children become quickly frustrated when they cannot use their hands to hold the objects down. You may want to discuss with them what happens when a bird encounters the same type of problem.

Answer Key For Questions:
1. Answers will vary. For example, each bird is able to get the type of food it needs to survive.
2. Answers will vary.
3. The beak enables the bird to feed on specific foods.

Literature Links:
Cannon, J. *Stellaluna*. Harcourt Brace, 1993.
Gans, R. *Bird Talk*. Thomas Y. Crowell, 1971.
Jeunesse, G. *Birds*. Scholastic, 1990.
Simon, N. *Benjy's Bird*. Albert Whitman, 1965.
Smucker, A. E. *Outside the Window*. Alfred A. Knopf, 1994.
Waddell, M. *Owl Babies*. Candlewick Press, 1992.
Willis, N. C. *The Robins in Your Backyard*. Cucumber Island Storytellers, 1996.

Portals for Expansion:

Mathematics
• Create a graph that represents trials versus successful captures of food for each of the types of bird beaks and each type of food.

Science
• Describe how a bird of prey's beak looks. This type of bird has a very sharp beak for tearing apart its food.
• Investigate the different types of birds of prey and what they eat.

Language Arts
• Write a story or poem from the perspective of the bird who is trying to catch its food. An example might be a woodpecker who is pecking away on a tree in search of insects.

Art
• Create a diorama of a bird actually searching for its food. Make sure the food and beak type are correct.

Name _____

The Shape of a Bird's Beak

Procedure: 1. Investigate to find out which "beak" is the best choice for picking up each "food" in the pan. Kinds of "beaks" provided:
  • pliers or tweezers for a long, narrow beak
  • clothespin for a triangular or squared off beak
  • spoon for a larger beak that is able to scoop up food
  • straw or coffee stirrer for a thin, narrow beak
2. Do not use your hands to hold anything except the "beak." Carefully touch the surrounding parts of the food such as the egg carton and soda bottle with the "beak."
3. Tell how you collected each type of food.

Food	"Beak" Used
beads (seeds)	
cotton balls (berries)	
plastic fish	
egg carton (tree with insects in bark)	
soda bottle (trumpet-shaped flowers)	

4. Draw the different types of beaks below.

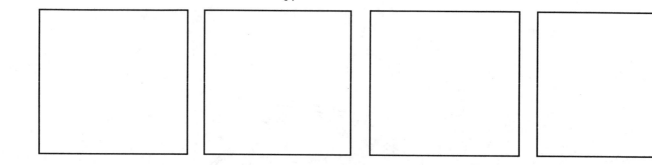

Name a bird that has a beak like this:

_____ _____ _____ _____

Kinds of food eaten by each type of bird:

_____ _____ _____ _____

Questions: _Answer the questions on the back of the paper._
1. Why is it important that birds have differently shaped beaks?
2. Describe a type of bird you see in your area. What kind of beak does that bird have? What foods does it eat?
3. How is the shape of a bird's beak a special adaptation?

THE HUMAN BODY & HEALTH

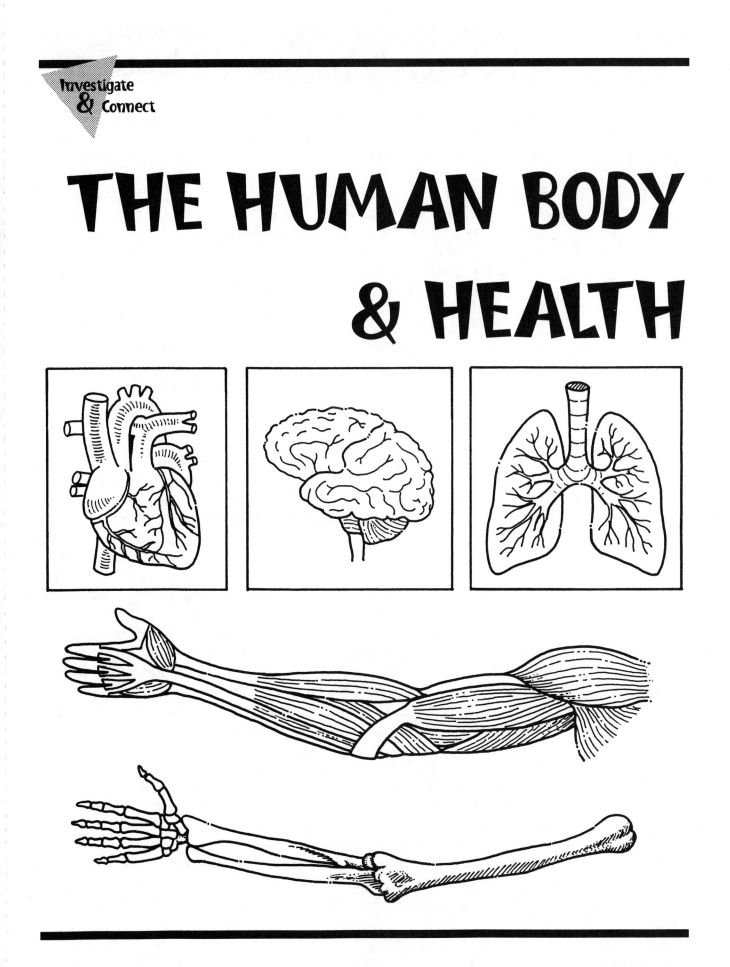

The Anatomy

The human animal is referred to as the highest level of living thing due to its complexity and its well-developed thought processes. The human animal section will not attempt to become a human anatomy and physiology text, but will seek to introduce systems in a way that permits comparison to the other animals discussed in earlier sections of this book. The human animal has eleven systems as follows: the integumentary system (skin and related structures), the skeletal system (bones, ligaments, and cartilage), the muscular system (for movement), the nervous system (senses, brain, spinal cord, and other nerves), the endocrine system (all hormone-producing glands), the digestive system (all organs related to processing nutrients), the respiratory system (lungs and airways), the circulatory system (heart and all related vessels and blood), the lymphatic system (thymus gland, spleen, lymph fluid, vessels, and nodes), the urinary system (kidneys, bladder, and related structures), and the reproductive system (testes in males, ovaries in females, and all related structures). A brief description of each system, some of the structures, and their functions will be reviewed.

The Integumentary System

The integumentary system includes the elastic body covering of skin. It is a membrane that keeps the body separate from its surroundings, protects against materials easily leaching from the body, and insures that the outside environment is kept outside of the body. Skin is not uniform over the entire body. At the fingertips nerve density is very high, making the fingertips one of the most sensitive areas of the body. The skin is stretched tight across the forearms, yet is not tight around the elbows to allow movement. The skin is formed of millions of tiny cells. It is estimated that all cells of the skin are replaced at least once each month. The integumentary system also includes hair, nails, and sweat glands. The hair and sweat glands assist the skin in maintaining a steady body temperature. When cold strikes the skin, the familiar "goose bumps" serve to raise the hair, keeping a layer of warmer air next to the skin. When very warm surroundings threaten to raise the body's temperature, the sweat glands operate to release water. As the water evaporates, it takes heat away from the body. This temperature regulating function is important for the survival of the individual.

The skin consists of several layers. The outside layer, the *epidermis,* is a layer of flat, dead cells. Melanin, which darkens the skin, is produced in special living cells deep in this layer. Going deeper, the next layer is the *dermis.* This is the layer in which nerves are present that allow the senses of touch and pain. This is also where *blood vessels, hair follicles,* and *sweat glands* exist. *Sebaceous* glands produce an oil that helps the skin stay soft, pliable, and waterproof. The dermis is supported by a layer of fat cells which serves to both insulate the body and store the energy-laden fat cells. A system of tiny ridges and valleys are established in the skin even before birth. Although the skin is replaced frequently, this pattern of ridges and valleys, especially visible in the skin of the fingers, maintains a unique fingerprint for each individual that lasts an entire lifetime.

The Skin

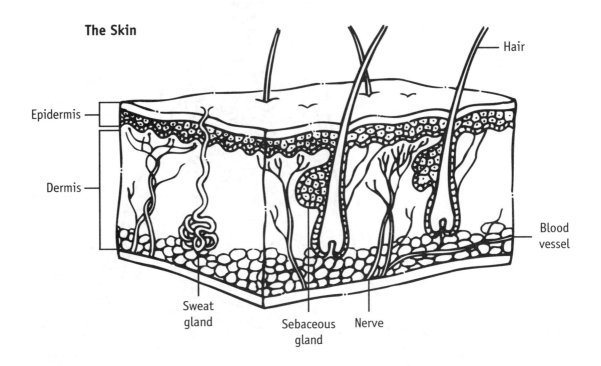

The Skeletal System

See Teacher Demonstration: "Types of Joints"

The skeletal system is the arrangement of bones, ligaments, and cartilage that holds and cushions the bones in place. Not all bones are the same size or shape. The smallest bones of the body are the three bones in the ear (the hammer, anvil, and stirrup) that connect the eardrum to the sensing nerves for sound. Other bones such as the femur (thigh bone) are large, and still others like those in the skull are flat. Although the bones look inanimate, like pieces of hard concrete, they include living cells, nerves, and blood vessels. The hard outer layer of a bone is only a structural covering for the spongy core of cells. This outer layer contains living cells that can reproduce. This is how broken bones mend. The calcium salts contained in this layer make the bone hard. The spongy material under the hard outer covering serves to make the bone strong, yet lightweight. The blood vessels contained within the bone surround and nourish the bone cells and connect with the bone marrow. The bone marrow is where red blood cells are made. Ligaments hold bones together at joints and cartilage cushions the bones in those joints that move. But not all joints do move. The joints of the skull bones are immovable, the bones that make up the vertebral column are only slightly movable, and the long bones of the extremities are very movable.

The Human Skeleton

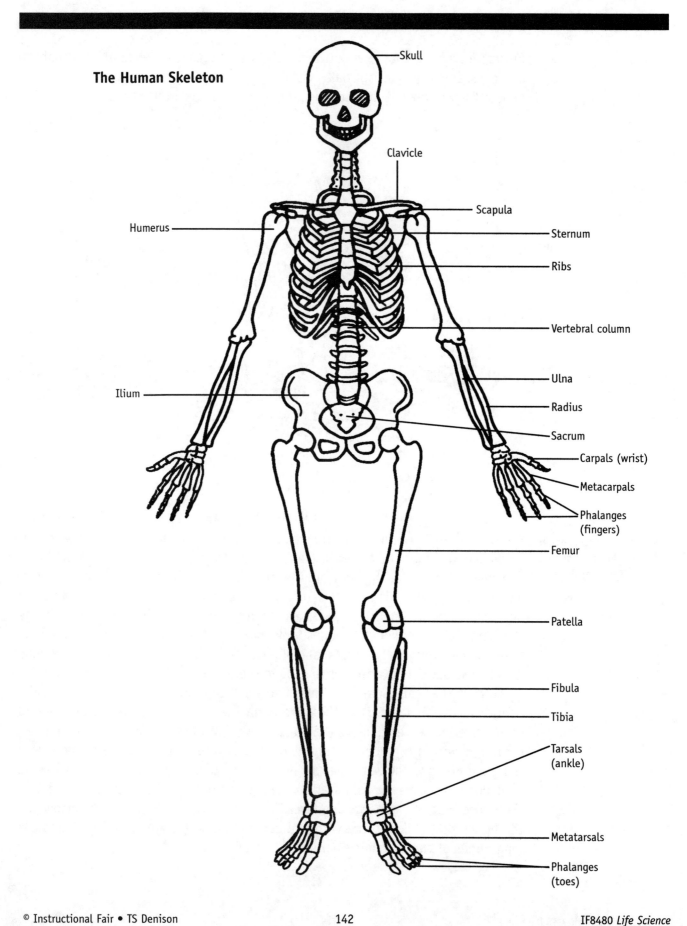

Skull

Clavicle

Scapula

Humerus

Sternum

Ribs

Vertebral column

Ulna

Ilium

Radius

Sacrum

Carpals (wrist)

Metacarpals

Phalanges (fingers)

Femur

Patella

Fibula

Tibia

Tarsals (ankle)

Metatarsals

Phalanges (toes)

The Muscular System

The muscular system is most known for the voluntary muscles. They include such muscles as the biceps and triceps. The biceps draw the forearm toward the upper arm when they are tightened. The triceps straighten the arm by pulling the forearm away from the upper arm. Yet there must be cooperation as the muscles train to work, for the triceps cannot effectively tighten if the biceps are also tightening. Biceps work while the triceps relax, and visa versa. Muscle cells are long and thin, forming a bundle of cells attached to bones with tendons. Some muscles are large, but others are small and delicate. The musculature of the face is among the most complex. If there is any doubt, try to wink one eye at a time. If that is successful, do the one eyebrow raise made famous by the television character Mister Spock of "Star Trek." Involuntary muscles are, in many ways, more important than the voluntary muscles. One cannot survive if the muscle of the heart does not rhythmically contract to pump blood throughout the body. The body cannot live if the smooth involuntary muscles of the digestive system do not work to extract energy from the food fed to it. Yet many people live healthy and productive lives with a variety of disabilities in voluntary muscles, such as limited or no function in the leg muscles.

The Nervous System

See Portal for Exploration "Reaction Time"

The nervous system includes a system of nerves running throughout the body and connected to the spinal cord. The function of the nerves is to pick up stimuli from the outside world as well as from inside the body and to carry those messages to the brain through the spinal cord. The brain, the body's message and control center, generates signals of its own that are sent back through the system of nerves to various areas of the body. The brain is made of three main parts: the brain stem, the cerebrum, and the cerebellum. The brain stem (*medulla*) controls signals that drive the involuntary muscles, such as those for breathing and keeping the heart beating. The *cerebellum* is the orchestrator that coordinates movement, as a director coordinates the actions of individual musicians. It is the cerebellum that coordinates the movements involved in walking and talking, for example. The *cerebrum* is divided into many sections that are the centers of the senses and intelligence as well as personality.

See Portal for Exploration "Recognizing Coins"

See Portal for Exploration "Map Your Tongue"

Nerve cells have an interesting structure and are uniquely designed to pass small electrical charges from one to the next. The cell has a central cell body that gathers in electrical impulses through the branching dendrites. They reach out for the electrical pulse as roots reach out for water. The long axon acts like an antenna with very thin terminal ends from which electrical impulses are transmitted. The transmission of electricity across the gaps between axons and the next dendrite still allows nerve signals to travel in excess of 240 kilometers per hour. The nerves fire an electrical impulse from a variety of stimuli. Light, heat, sound, touch, smell, taste, and other stimuli affect certain nerves that travel a specific pathway to a particular region in the brain. When the sense is transmitted to the brain, the brain may fire back a response. For example, bright light is sensed, the pupil shrinks. The light reflection from a specific word causes a corresponding image to form in the brain. Pain is simply a strong, uncomfortable stimulus that causes a reaction. The finger touches a hot iron, and the arm recoils away. A loud sound causes the person to turn his/her head away. The strong odor of a skunk causes a person to keep his/her distance.

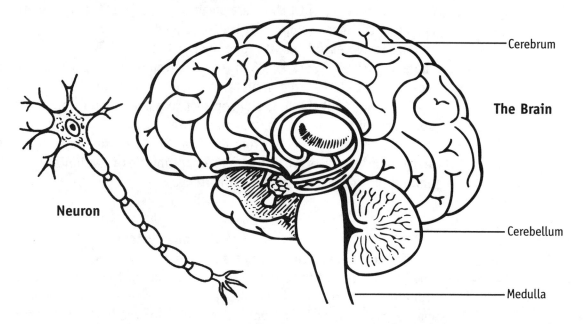

Neuron

Cerebrum

The Brain

Cerebellum

Medulla

The Endocrine System

The endocrine system consists of all hormone-producing glands that assist in the control of the life processes, or metabolism. This includes the pituitary, thyroid, parathyroid, adrenal glands, and the pancreas. The pituitary, located at the base of the brain, is best known for the release of the growth hormone. It also produces a hormone that stimulates the thyroid gland. The thyroid gland is located in the neck and controls the metabolic rate of cells, the production of protein, and utilization of the lipids by the body. It also helps in controlling the calcium and phosphate content of blood. The parathyroid is attached to the thyroid and can cause blood calcium to increase. The adrenal glands are located on top of the kidneys. They produce epinephrine and norepinephrine, generally referred to as the "fight or flight" hormones. They prepare the body for energy-expending action. The pancreas is attached to the small intestine and is as important to digestion as it is to the endocrine system. Insulin is produced by the islets of Langerhans and is responsible for moving glucose into cells to regularte metabolism. High blood sugar levels result if insulin levels are too low. Other glands in this system are responsible for producing of melatonin, lymphocytes, sex hormones, and digestive hormones.

The Digestive System

The digestive system includes the mouth, esophagus, stomach, small intestine, large intestine, rectum, and anus. In the *mouth*, the teeth and jaws physically break down food while saliva moistens the material for an easier passage down the esophagus. An enzyme in saliva begins the chemical breakdown of starch into sugars, an effect that can be detected by a sweet taste resulting from holding a cracker in the mouth for a period of time. The rhythmic movement of the *esophagus* forces the food into the *stomach*. Powerful acids and enzymes churn the food and accelerate the chemical breakdown of the food into usable nutrients. The mixture then moves into the *small intestine* where the nutrients pass into the bloodstream. Bile, created by the *liver*, is stored in the gall bladder until it is needed for the digestion of fats inside the small intestine. The *pancreas* produces enzymes for use inside the small intestine as well. They break down carbohydrates, proteins, and fats into chemicals that can be used by the body. Water is extracted from the remnants as it passes through the *large intestine*. The waste is stored in the *rectum* until muscles are contracted and the waste material is released through the anus. The digestive system represents a continuous opening, controlled by a number of valves, clear through the body. Much of the system contains very active digestive juices that must be separated from the walls of the organs by a specialized protective layer of mucus.

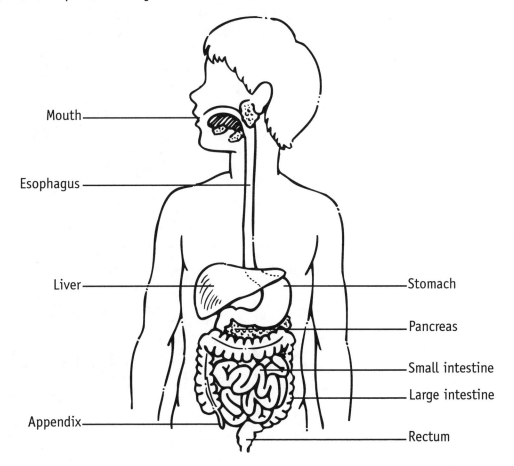

The Respiratory System

The respiratory system includes the mouth and nasal cavities, the larynx, the trachea, the bronchial tubes, and the lungs. The diaphragm is a muscle found below the lungs that is very important in the operation of the respiratory system. It draws the lung downward, lowering the air pressure in the lungs. This lower pressure causes the air from outside the body to rush into the lungs as they are explanded. Air is taken in through the mouth or *nasal cavities* and is drawn down the *trachea* into the *bronchial tubes*. The bronchial tubes lead to the *lungs* where the *bronchioles* branch out to very small air sacs called *alveoli*. The alveoli are lined with capillaries and are the site of gas exchange. Blood having low oxygen and high carbon dioxide levels is pumped from the heart to the lungs where it absorbs more oxygen and gives off carbon dioxide. The oxygenated blood returns to the heart through the pulmonary vein to be circulated through the heart to the rest of the body. As the diaphragm moves upward squeezing the lungs into a smaller volume, the air is forced by higher pressure to the comparatively lower pressure outside the body. As the air passes through the larynx, vocal cords can produce the noise we call voice. Not all of the oxygen in the air is absorbed by the blood in the alveoli, nor is all of the carbon dioxide given off. The exhaled air has a little less oxygen and a little more carbon dioxide. It is not, as popular belief may have it, pure carbon dioxide. The technique of mouth-to-mouth respiration would make little sense if it were.

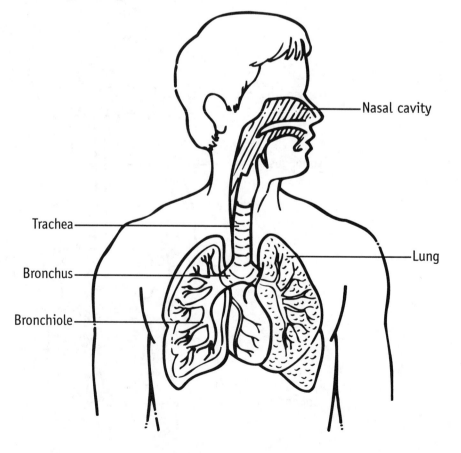

Nasal cavity

Trachea

Bronchus

Bronchiole

Lung

The Circulatory System

The circulatory system includes the blood, the heart, and all related vessels that carry and distribute the blood. The blood consists of several parts. A liquid called plasma is the material that carries red blood cells, white blood cells, and platelets. Red blood cells are red due to the presence of hemoglobin, the compound that carries oxygen to the far reaches of the body. White blood cells are the police of the body, protecting against infection from foreign agents. Platelets assist in the maintenance of the body by thickening blood and causing clotting. The four chambered heart is the muscle that pumps the blood through the body. The blood is contained in arteries as it leaves the heart, and in veins as it returns to the heart. As the blood travels through the arteries, they begin to branch into smaller and smaller vessels until the blood is finally directed through the capillaries. These very small, thin vessels, nearly a red blood cell in diameter, are where the greatest amount of exchange of oxygen and other nutrients takes place.

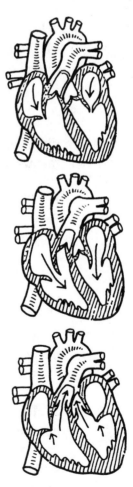

The heart is a complex pump. It accepts oxygen-poor blood from the body into the right atrium and pushes it to the right ventricle. From there the blood is pushed through the pulmonary arteries to the lungs for oxygenation. The pulmonary veins accept the oxygenated blood from the lungs and return it to the heart. The oxygenated blood enters the left atrium where it is pushed into the left ventricle. Attached to the left ventricle is the aorta that begins the distribution to many important arteries that will carry the oxygenated blood throughout the body. The passage of blood into, out of, and through the heart is controlled by a series of valves that operate for the one-way flow of blood. The beat, or squeezing of the heart, occurs about 70 times each minute, but can be influenced by exercise. The pulse in your arm (radial pulse) or neck (carotid pulse) is felt when the blood pressure increases as the heart squeezes the blood out toward the distant points of the body.

See Portal for Exploration "Pulse Rate"

The Lymphatic System

The lymphatic system helps to maintain a balance between the fluids as they pass between tissues and the blood. More fluid is lost by the blood than is returned, thus causing a buildup of fluid in the tissues. The lymphatic system provides the function of eliminating that fluid so that a net increase of fluids in the tissues cannot happen. A system of lymph capillaries collect this extra fluid, and they merge into lymph vessels. Lymph vessels lead to specialized organs called lymph nodes, and many vessels form lymph trunks after leaving the lymph nodes. The lymph trunks join one of two lymph ducts and enter the venous flow, becoming part of the plasma just before it enters the heart. The lymph vessels completes another function in that it carries invading bacterial or other foreign microbes to the lymph nodes. Large numbers of lymphocytes reside in the lymph nodes and act to destroy those foreign bodies that may threaten the health of the person. The thymus is also a part of the lymph system and is the site for the production of the body's T-lymphocytes that provide the body with immunity. The spleen is the largest of the lymphatic organs and serves a specified function to rid the body of old, dying red blood cells as they squeeze through the thin walls of blood capillaries in the spleen.

The Urinary System

The urinary system is responsible for the elimination of liquid wastes and the dissolved salts the wastes carry. The kidneys (normally a pair in each individual) remove waste products from the blood stream. The kidney also helps to control the volume, composition, and pH of bodily fluids. These are the functions that the kidneys serve, and the result is the formation of urine. Urine is carried by a thin tube called the ureter to the urinary bladder. It stores the urine until it is released through the urethra to the outside. A function of this system is to assist in the balance between water and the dissolved salts in the body. These salts, electrolytes, are important if electrical impulses are to travel between neurons in the nervous system. The balance between enough, insufficient, and too many electrolytes is a very fragile balance. The existence of a suitable environment for growth is a delicate balance often called homeostasis, and the urinary system is important in its maintenance.

The Reproductive System

The reproductive system of the human animal is sexual with individuals possessing the structures of only one sex. The female has ovaries that produce eggs that burst from follicles during ovulation. The release of the egg also stimulates the production of estrogen and progesterone responsible for readying the lining of the uterus for possible pregnancy. The egg is carried by the fallopian tube to the uterus. If fertilization by a sperm cell takes place, the fertilized cell implants on the blood-rich surface of the uterus, and a pregnancy results. If fertilization and implantation do not occur, a sharp decrease in the female hormones estrogen and progesterone cause a sloughing off of the uterine lining. The cellular debris and associated blood are carried through the cervix and vagina to be eliminated as a menstrual flow (menses). The process of maturing follicles, ovulation, pregnancy, or menses continues on a cycle of approximately 28 days from onset of puberty to middle age.

In the male, sperm and testosterone are produced in two egg-shaped testes contained within a sac called the scrotum. The scrotum is located outside the body which allows for better temperature control. The sperm is stored in the epididymis, a long tube that gathers immature sperm from the testes. The vas deferens, a long tube that reaches to the prostate gland, allows the sperm to mature. The vas deferens unites with the seminal vesicle which produces a fluid that regulates the pH of the mixture, including sperm, to be carried to the outside. The prostate secretes a fluid that also acts to balance pH as well as increasing the motility of sperm cells. The semen, the fluid containing the sperm, is conveyed to the outside through the urethra, emerging from the penis during ejaculation. Should the sperm reach an egg and cause fertilization, pregnancy results.

Health and Nutrition

The care and feeding of the human body is a complex subject. If the human animal eats too much and does not exercise properly the results may be major health problems. These health issues are each a major focus of industry with billions of dollars each year spent on diet products, exercise programs, and equipment. This treatment of the subject will not attempt to cover the entire content and all of the intricate implications, but will establish the basics. Some individuals may have unique needs brought about by their own bodily functions and complexities. The statements made in this section are general rules of thumb and not intended to become a guide for a specific individual's diet.

In nutrition, there are five areas for consideration. The nutrients include carbohydrates, proteins, lipids, vitamins, and water. The value of water is obvious and is the most critical need for the survival of the individual. One may survive for extended times without the other nutrients, but survival is only a matter of days without water.

Vitamins are materials that are necessary for the ongoing metabolic processes and cannot be produced by the human animal. There are, in broad terms, six essential vitamins. They include the water-soluble vitamins B and C, and the fat-soluble vitamins A, D, E, and K. The difference between these groups of vitamins is that the body will store the fat-soluble vitamins, while the body will release the water-soluble vitamins in urine. An excess of fat-soluble vitamins may be unhealthy, so supplementation is not common. An adequate amount of these vitamins are normally found in a well-balanced diet. Vitamin D, for example, is often added to milk in order to assist with the absorption of calcium contained in the milk. Additional supplements of vitamin D are normally not needed. The water-soluble vitamins B and C are regularly supplemented. Vitamin B, actually a number of different compounds together referred to as the "B complex," assists in the regulation of cellular metabolism. Vitamin C is also responsible for some degree of regulation of cellular metabolism, but is popularly known for its effects on the general health of the individual and its ability to fight the common cold.

See Portal for Exploration "Testing Foods"

Carbohydrates are polysaccharides (molecules made from complex combinations of simple sugars) that are broken down by the digestive system into monosaccharides (simple sugars) that provide a majority of the energy needs of the human body. Carbohydrates include the sugars fructose, galactose, and glucose. These simple sugars can be released by the digestive process and used by the body. Cellulose, a polysaccharide plentiful in plants, cannot be digested by the human animal. As a result, it will supply none of the energy necessary for the survival of the animal, but it does serve an important function. Commonly referred to as "roughage," or "fiber," the cellulose provides bulk as it passes, largely unchanged, through the digestive system. The benefits to the system include a cleansing effect as the muscles of the digestive system are provided with a firm material. Carbohydrates may also be used to produce the complex sugars ribose and deoxyribose, necessary for the production of DNA and RNA. Most carbohydrates, however, are directed toward energy production. It is estimated that from 100 to 125 grams of protein are needed (specific needs of the individual vary widely with energy requirements) to stop the body from beginning to produce the needed saccharide glucose from its reservoir of protein.

Proteins are the structural components that build cells and regulate metabolism as enzymes. An enzyme is a molecule that allows a chemical process to occur. For instance, the enzyme amylase in saliva permits the chemical process of breaking down complex sugars into simple sugars. Amylase is, in fact, a digestive enzyme and, therefore, a protein. The materials that build proteins are called amino acids. It is important to note that eight of the twenty-one amino acids cannot be produced by the human body and must be obtained through diet. These eight amino acids are identified as the essential amino acids. As protein is digested, the amino acids are released. They are reassembled into other proteins to be used as structural protein, enzymes, hormones, or the protein found in plasma. Alternatively, they can be used for the production of energy or in the production of glucose or fat. Rich sources of protein include milk, fish, poultry, red meat, and eggs. Plant materials may be lacking some essential amino acids. Beans, for instance, supply the essential amino acids that rice is lacking. Thus, rice and beans become a creative combination of plants that can supply the vegetarian with a sufficient amount of all essential amino acids.

Fat is a term widely applied to the entire class of materials named the lipids. The lipids include fatty acids, triglycerides, and cholesterol. As the fat intake by the human body is digested, the triglycerides are converted to glycerol and fatty acids. The fatty acids may be converted by the liver into other fatty acids, one of which, linoleic acid, is considered essential. It is required to build phospholipid, a necessary component of cell membranes. The liver is the organ most responsible for the control of the amount and form of the fat in the body. It is the liver that can control the amount of triglyceride and cholesterol in the bloodstream. While some of these materials are necessary for the body, excessive amounts of fat are known to be a health hazard. Yet fats are important in that they also carry the fat-soluble vitamins with them. However, it is recommended that fat in the adult diet supply less than 30% of the calories needed to maintain the human body.

The human animal sits at the top of the food chain. Individuals may choose to be vegetarian, but the human is born as a predator. It can survive as an herbivore, but is, more commonly, an omnivore, eating both plant and animal material to sustain life. What is a problem in the lives of many human animals is a lack of exercise. Most especially in the lives of those who lead sedentary lifestyles, like writers and college professors, a conscious effort must be made to exercise. It is exercise that will keep up the level of metabolism necessary for a healthy life. If exercise is not a feature of life, and the amount of food does not decrease, then a weight gain may place undue stress on many of the body's systems. The liver may forced to work hard in an effort to control a fat-rich diet. Excess fat entering the bloodstream may precipitate to form a coating on the inner surfaces of the blood vessels, raising blood pressure and reducing the vessels normally pliable nature. Appropriate attention to the diet and to maintaining some form of exercise program is essential for the long-term survival of the human.

Personal and Public Health

Illness in the human animal can result from many different situations. Environmental factors such as chemical air and water pollution can cause illness. Acids in air pollution can cause a burning sensation in the eyes and other gases can cause difficulty in respiration. Many deaths each year are caused by unhealthy levels of pollution in the air some humans breathe. Accidents are also a source of death and discomfort. Traumatic injuries in accidents caused over 48,000 deaths in the United States in 1996 alone. Natural disasters are also a source of human injury and death. Weather and geologic events are often forecasted, yet the denial of frailty often leads a number of human animals to die rather than take shelter or evacuate. As pollution laws are enforced, as automobile safety becomes increasingly important, and as natural disasters become better forecasted, these sources of human suffering will be reduced.

Nutrition may also be a source of human illness. Malnutrition is caused by a diet that supplies an insufficient amount of calories for energy, or essential lipids, essential amino acids, and vitamins or minerals for proper maintenance of the human body. Every year 13-18 million people die from the effects of hunger and starvation. The average dog in North America eats more food calories each day than the average person in India. One in five people on planet Earth suffer from chronic hunger. Not all malnutrition is caused by undernutrition. While undernutrition is a problem in many parts of the world, and, indeed, in parts of the United States, malnutrition can be a problem simply due to the necessary or voluntary choice of diet. No matter the palate, a diet sufficient for proper nutrition in the United States should be easily possible.

See Portal for Exploration "Bacteria Hunt"

Most human illnesses, however, are caused by bacteria, viruses, and cancer. Cancer is a name applied to a variety of disorders that result in unnatural cell reproduction. This can include the uncontrolled cell division that develops into malignant tumors, as well as the development of a large scale invasion of entire body systems. Bacteria are very small, one-celled organisms that may have very serious effects on individuals. Some bacteria are normally found in nature, and some are even found inside the human body. However, if the bacteria not normally associated with a particular part of the human animal invade and begin to flourish, illness results. The bacteria E. coli, for example, lives in the human intestine. If it enters the upper digestive system, it can cause dysentery, a particularly unpleasant illness. Visitors to foreign lands may be familiar with this disease as "Montezuma's revenge." Other bacteria not normally part of the human animal can cause infections of the throat (strep throat) and of the lungs (bacterial pneumonia). Many bacterial infections are fought off by the body's own defense network; especially in the lymphatic system, specialized cells attack and destroy foreign biologic invaders. Some infections of bacterial origin may overwhelm the body's defense network, but most can be cured with drugs known as antibiotics.

As the name implies, this class of drug is capable of working against life, and hopefully, can kill the infection without doing too much damage to the rest of the human body.

See Portal for Exploration "Epidemic"

Viral infection is a particular concern to the human body, for natural defenses are often not in place to combat the viruses, and antibiotics are not effective in fighting them. If natural immunity is not present, the individual simply must rely on the body adapting to the condition by generating new defenses (antibodies) before the virus unbalances the individual's systems too badly. Antibodies may be artificially built up against specific viral infections in the inoculation process. An injection of a small amount of a particular virus causes the body to begin to create antibodies to fight off the foreign invaders. Although the injection of material is small, the body creates a storehouse of the antibodies capable of fighting off subsequent infections by that virus. Some viruses, however, are not effectively defeated by the body's defenses. The HIV virus, the virus that leads to AIDS, has no known vaccine. Other viruses, some forms of hemorrhagic fever, for example, are capable of running through an entire population, unchecked. Research aimed at developing weapons to fight these diseases is ongoing.

Systems for the promotion of public health have been established to fight large outbreaks of disease, and they work to control those that do occur. In addition, departments of public health monitor some areas of individual health closely for the benefit of all individuals in a social arrangement. Outbreaks of tuberculosis still occur in the United States, but reports to departments of public health have resulted in controlling what was once a large-scale killer. Public health efforts made as far back as 30 to 40 years have controlled polio and smallpox. These fatal or debilitating diseases are now very rare in countries with an active public health program. Similar efforts are now under way to try to increase the number of children inoculated against childhood diseases both in this country and around the world. Research continues, worldwide, for cures to viral infections we do not know how to cure, and for the secret that is responsible for the triggering of the many forms of cancer. As we learn more, the general health of the human animal population of this planet will benefit.

Portals for Learning: Literature

Aliki. *My Five Senses*. Thomas Y. Crowell, 1989.
A book for younger readers, it presents the five senses and ways they can be used.

Aliki. *I'm Growing!* HarperCollins, 1992.
This book describes what happens to your body as it grows.

Arnau, E. *The Skeletal System*. Chelsea House, 1995.
This book would serve as an excellent reference book on the skeletal system for older readers. The skeletal system and bones are explained through illustrations and in-depth text.

Balestrino, P. *The Skeleton Inside You*. Thomas Y. Crowell, 1989.
The reader is introduced to 206 bones in the human body, their characteristics, and their ability to mend themselves when damaged.

Barrett, J. *Cloudy with a Chance of Meatballs*. Aladdin Books, 1978.
The weather in this town of Chewandswallow is various forms of food. This would be a good book to discuss balanced meals since every meal is provided by precipitation.

Bell, S., & Parsons, A. (eds.) *What's Inside My Body?* Dorling Kindersley, 1991.
A book for young children, it explains the body's systems and the organs' functions. Also provided are illustrations and photographs of people to explain the information clearly.

Berger, M. *Germs Make Me Sick*. Thomas Y. Crowell, 1985.
This Lets-Read-and-Find-Out science book explains how bacteria and viruses make the human body sick and how the body fights them off.

Cole, J. *The Magic School Bus Inside the Human Body*. Scholastic, 1989.
Ms. Frizzle takes her class on a field trip inside the human body to explore various organs and systems.

Cole, J. *Your Insides*. Putnam and Grosset, 1992.
This book helps the reader examine the different parts of the body and how they interact with each other. The book provides sections of information on various topics, such as the brain, blood, each system and its organs.

Ehlert, L. *Eating the Alphabet: Fruits and Vegetables from A to Z*. Harcourt Brace Jovanovich, 1989.
The reader is taken on a tour of the alphabet using vegetables and fruits to illustrate each letter. This book could be used for a discussion on choosing healthful fruits and vegetables.

Kates, B. J. *We're Different, We're the Same*. Random House, 1992.
Using Jim Henson's Muppets from Sesame Street, this book shows that people have the same body parts but they can vary according to the individual.

May, J., & Stevenson, J. *The Magic School Bus Inside Ralphie*. Scholastic, 1995.
A series spin-off from the television show, this book has Ms. Frizzle taking a trip inside of Ralphie who stayed home because he is feeling ill. The field trip helps the students understand information about germs and the body's defense mechanisms against them.

Nottridge, R. *Fats*. Carolrhoda, 1992.
This book introduces the different types of fats that are consumed, identifying those which are helpful or harmful to the human body. This reference book may be used for discussing healthful foods and the consequences of too much fat in a diet.

Nottridge, R. *Sugars*. Carolrhoda, 1992.
A factual book, it discusses how sugars enter the diet and how the body processes the different types of sugars.

Parker, S. *Eating a Meal: How You Eat, Drink, and Digest*. Franklin Watts, 1991.
The reader is introduced to the digestive system. The book provides clear illustrations and text that describes the process of digesting food in the body.

Parker, S. *Human Body*. Dorling Kindersley, 1993.
An encyclopedia-type book for older readers, there is a great deal of technical information and helpful illustrations on various topics about the human body.

Parker, S. *Look at Your Body Skeleton*. Copper Beech Books, 1996.
This book explains the different types of joints, the skeleton, and diseases of the bones.

Parramon, M. *How Our Blood Circulates*. Chelsea House, 1994.
The reader learns about the circulatory system. The book explains how blood is pumped from the heart throughout the rest of the body. Additional information is given about the nutrients and minerals carried by the blood.

Patent, D. H. *Germs!* Holiday House, 1983.
This book describes germs and how they attack the body. Additional information is given on how the body fights back and about immunizations that fight germs.

Richardson, J. *What Happens when You Catch a Cold?* Gareth Stevens, 1984.
The reader is given information on how the body fights off a cold using natural resources like blood cells and antibodies.

Roca, N., & Serrano, M. *The Respiratory System*. Chelsea House, 1996.
An informational book, it provides detailed information on the respiratory system. Through illustrations and text, the reader learns how the lungs take in oxygen and how it is distributed throughout the body.

Sandeman, A. *Blood*. Brookfield, CT: Copper Beech Books, 1996.
This book explains what blood is and its function in the human body. Using illustrations, the reader learns how blood helps bruises heal and carries nutrients to parts of the body.

Schuman, B. N. *The Human Eye*. Atheneum, 1968.
Although dated, this book is a good reference on the human eye. It provides illustrations and text that describe how the human eye works.

Showers, P. *Hear Your Heart*. Thomas Y. Crowell, 1968.
An older book, it provides good information on how the heart pumps blood throughout the body, its structure, and the pulse rate.

Simon, S. *Bones: Our Skeletal System*. Morrow Junior Books, 1998.
Through illustrations and photographs, the skeletal system and its functions are discussed.

Simon, S. *Muscles: Our Muscular System*. Morrow Junior Books, 1998.
Through illustrations and computer-enhanced photographs, the muscular system and its functions, types of muscles found in the human body, and how exercise affects muscles are discussed.

Vincent, G. *Feel Better, Ernest!* Greenwillow, 1988.
Celestine, a mouse, takes care of Ernest when he is sick in bed. The book is useful when discussing what to do to get over a cold.

Ward, B. R. *The Eye and Seeing*. Franklin Watts, 1981.
This book provides information on the physical structure of the eye and how it sees. Vocabulary words are in bold print and the text provides much information for the reader in a simple and understandable manner.

Wright, L. *Hearing*. Raintree Steck Vaughn, 1995.
An informational story that provides answers to questions about the sense of hearing. There is a table of contents page and index section that directs the students to specific information.

Wright, L. *Seeing*. Raintree Steck Vaughn, 1995.
An informational story, the book provides answers to questions about the sense of sight. There is a table of contents page and index section that directs the students to specific information.

Wright, L. *Smelling and Tasting*. Raintree Steck Vaughn, 1995.
This informational book provides answers to questions about the senses of taste and smell. There is a table of contents page and index section that directs the students to specific information.

Types of Joints

Teacher Demonstration

Purpose:
- Identify the differences among the three major types of joints between bones in the body.
- Describe how the type of joint affects the amount and kind of movement that is permitted.

Materials Needed:
2 pencils
5 cm of clear, flexible plastic aquarium tubing
pieces of a discarded puzzle
4 wood blocks (play set)
3 pieces of foam rubber (same size as the blocks, half as thick)
school glue
waxed paper

Introduction: The places where bones meet are called joints. Some joints have a larger range of movement than others. The three major types of joints in the body are movable, immovable, and partially movable. Movable joints, modeled by the extremities, such as the ankles, can be further classified by range of movement: hinge (finger, knee, elbow), ball and socket (hip and shoulder), and pivot (rotate forearm, wrist, neck). The immovable joint to be modeled is the joint between the portions of bone that make up the skull. The partially movable joint to be modeled is that series of joints or gliding joints that make up the backbone, or vertebral column.

Procedure:
1. Place two pencils into the ends of the flexible plastic tubing.
2. Show how this type of joint can permit a range of movement—back and forth and rotation.
3. Using school glue, adhere several pieces of discarded puzzle together on a sheet of waxed paper. This provides a model for immovable joints, formed by bones in the skull.
4. Discuss how some bones of the skeleton (the skull) cannot fuse until they grow together. Indicate how the skull can be deformed until certain bones fuse. Obviously, during the birth process, this flexibility is beneficial, however these spaces or soft spots are also sites of particular concern as the child's body grows and develops.
5. Stack and glue the blocks and foam rubber in place in alternating fashion, block, foam, block, foam, block, foam, and block.
6. Demonstrate that the foam allows only a limited range of motion, such as the gliding joints in the vertebral column.
7. After the glue is dried, flex the model of the vertebral column numerous times to demonstrate how a variety of injuries to the "disk" material of foam and the joints they cushion can occur.

Literature Links:
Arnau, E. *The Skeletal System*. Chelsea House, 1995.
Balestrino, P. *The Skeleton Inside You*. Thomas Y. Crowell, 1989.
Parker, S. *Human Body*. Dorling Kindersley, 1993.
Parker, S. *Look at Your Body Skeleton*. Copper Beech Books, 1996.
Simon. S. *Bones: Our Skeletal System*. Morrow Junior Books, 1998.
Simon. S. *Muscles: Our Muscular System*. Morrow Junior Books, 1998.

Portals for Expansion:

Science
- Invite a medical professional to discuss the nature of injuries to the joints in the human body.
- Research to find out what types of athletic injuiries commonly occur.

Social Studies
- Discuss how U.S. historians of the Civil War are identifying skeletal remains of soldiers based on their individual characteristics.

Language Arts
- Write a report regarding cultural and individual differences that affect the health of joints, such as the difficulties often incurred by those studying the martial arts.

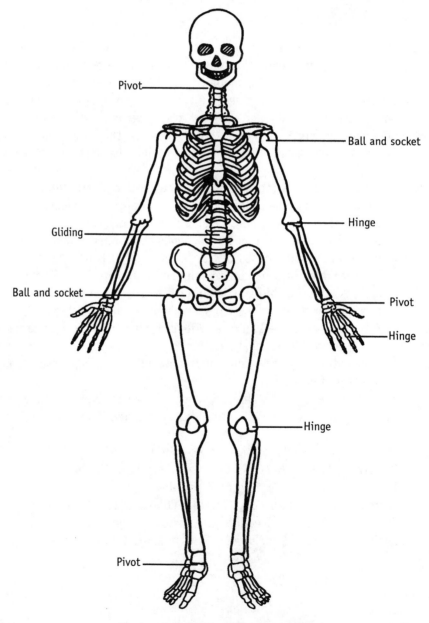

Types of Joints in the Body

What's Your Reaction Time?

Purpose:
- Define the term reaction time.
- Measure your own reaction time.

Materials Needed:
meter stick
calculator
pencil

Introduction: As video game players known, there is a delay from the time one detects a stimulus (something that one senses) to the time that one can react (response). The delay between stimulus and response is called the reaction time. The reaction time varies from one person to the next and may, in part, explain why some people are good at some games and sports, and why other people are not. This activity times the delay using a dropped meter stick (the stimulus) and measuring the delay in terms of the length of meter stick that is allowed to fall before the thumb and forefinger grips the meter stick (the response).

Procedure: See student lab sheet for instructions.

Answer Key For Questions:
1. The reaction time is shorter when a warning is issued.
2. The driver of a car needs to apply the brakes quickly to avoid collisions.
3. The driver's reaction time is better when riding in a quiet car because there are fewer distractions.

Literature Links:
Aliki. *My Five Senses*. Thomas Y. Crowell, 1989.
Cole, J. *Your Insides*. Putnam and Grosset, 1992.
Ward, B. R. *The Eye and Seeing*. Franklin Watts, 1981.

Portals for Expansion:

Mathematics
- Calculate how long the reaction time was knowing that the acceleration due to gravity is 980 cm/sec^2.
  Use the following formula: 2 x distance (in cm) ÷ 980 (acceleration of gravity) = time
- Calculate the distance covered by a bicycle traveling at 15 km/hr (6.7 m/sec) if the reaction time was one second, one half second, etc.
  Use the formula: distance = rate (6.7 m/sec) x time
- Calculate similar distances for a car traveling at 30 km/hr, 45 km/hr, and 60 km/hr.

Social Studies
- Discuss the effect of alcohol on reaction time, and "Driving Under the Influence" (DUI) laws that respond to the problem.
- Find examples of traffic and other signs that are intended to increase attention and reduce reaction time.

Language Arts
- Write a creative story or poem that addresses reaction time by telling about a family and their rules for traveling in a car.

Art
- Create a poster that warns of the effects of drugs and alcohol on reaction time.

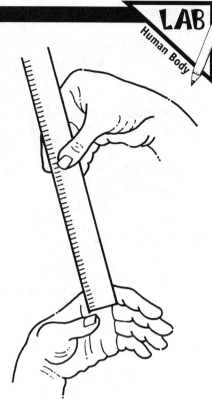

LAB

Human Body

What's Your Reaction Time?

Procedure: 1. While working with a partner, hold your finger and thumb of the same hand about 2-3 cm apart.

2. Have your partner hold a meter stick vertically so that the bottom edge is between your thumb and forefinger and it touches neither.

3. Do a countdown, and upon arriving at zero, the partner releases the meter stick while you clasp your finger and thumb to grab it.

4. Record the measurement at which the meter stick was stopped.

5. Repeat the exercise two more times, recording each trial. Calculate your average at the end.

6. Now do three trials without the countdown warning. The meter stick should be dropped while you and your partner tell a story or have a discussion.

7. Switch roles and test your partner's reaction time.

Reaction Time With Countdown

Trial 1 = _____ cm

Trial 2 = _____ cm

Trial 3 = _____ cm

Average: _____ cm

Reaction Time Without Countdown

Trial 1 = _____ cm

Trial 2 = _____ cm

Trial 3 = _____ cm

Average: _____ cm

Questions: _Answer the questions on the back of the paper._

1. In which situation, with or without warning, are reaction times shorter?

2. If a person is driving a car, when would reaction time be important?

3. Would reaction times be better in a quiet car or in a car with loud music and talking? Why?

Recognizing Coins

Purpose:
- Identify the importance of this sense by identifying coins only by touch.
- Recognize how accommodations can be made if some amount of sensation is blocked out.

Materials Needed:
shoe box
two of penny, nickel, dime, quarter
other coins: half dollar, dollar coins
pencil/pen

Introduction:
A significant portion of the brain is dedicated to the senses in the hand. Even though injuries to the hand may be relatively minor, the nerve density causes enormous pain. This activity examines how one's touch is accurate enough the identify coins.

Procedure:
1. See student lab sheet for instructions.
2. When finished, have students compare the accuracy using both hands to the accuracy using one hand.

Literature Links:
Aliki. *My Five Senses*. Thomas Y. Crowell, 1989.

Portals for Expansion:

Science
- Repeat the experiment using rubber surgical gloves simulating the loss of sensation that may accompany aging.

Social Studies
- Discuss why the Susan B. Anthony coin was discontinued in the United States as a replacement for the dollar bill.
- Discuss the value in creating coins in different sizes, materials, or with different edges.
- Talk about the impact of allowing each state/province to design a back for a coin thus producing many versions of the same coin.

Language Arts
- Write a poem or other creative work regarding the tasks that we do, or the objects we encounter each day, involving the sense of touch.

Art
- Draw large replicas or make rubbings of the coins for a collage. Include pictures that relate to money.
- Create a collage on paper or cardboard that utilizes a variety of textures provided by natural materials.

Name

Recognizing Coins

Procedure: 1. Have your partner place eight coins into the box without showing them to you.

2. Without looking at the coins, draw a coin from the box. *Do not look at it.* Have your partner record the type of coin by placing a checkmark in the corresponding box on the data sheet.

3. Again without looking at the coin, feel the coin with both hands and identify it.

4. Have your partner record the guess. If the guess is right, write a "+" above the checkmark. If incorrect, write a "–" in the space.

5. Continue until the box is empty.

6. Have your partner calculate the percentage of accuracy by dividing the number right by the total number of coins and then multiplying by 100.

Accuracy: _____

7. Change roles and repeat the exercise. Complete your partner's data sheet.

8. Do the activity again. This time use only one hand to identify the coins.

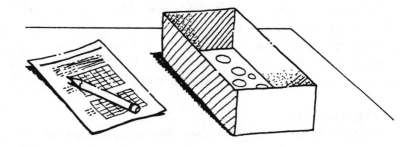

Recognizing Coins Data Sheet

LAB Invertebrates

Using Both Hands

	penny	nickel	dime	quarter	other	other
Coin #1						
Coin #2						
Coin #3						
Coin #4						
Coin #5						
Coin #6						
Coin #7						
Coin #8						

✓ Actual coin

+ Correct guess

– Incorrect guess

Using One Hand

	penny	nickel	dime	quarter	other	other
Coin #1						
Coin #2						
Coin #3						
Coin #4						
Coin #5						
Coin #6						
Coin #7						
Coin #8						

✓ Actual coin

+ Correct guess

– Incorrect guess

Map Your Tongue

Purpose:
- Illustrate the location of the senses on the human tongue by mapping the taste regions of sweet, sour, and salty.
- Describe what specific nerve cells are uniquely suited to sense specific stimuli.

Materials Needed:

cotton swabs	water
small paper cups	salt
lemon juice	sugar

Introduction: The tongue is a sense organ that has a very high nerve cell density. It is uniquely suited to taste, but not all of the nerve cells sense the same tastes. Some of the cells recognize sweetness, some identify sour tastes, and others identify saltiness. The location of each of these groups of nerves is fairly isolated, yielding regions on the tongue. The purpose of this activity is to have students locate these regions and to realize that all nerve cells do not accomplish all tasks. It is for this reason that the brain, although formed of nerve cells, may not sense pain. The spinal cord, although it may sense pain, may not sense light. Although the eyes sense pain and light, they cannot sense smell. Students will work in pairs for this activity. Safety concerns must be reviewed: have the students use separate cotton swabs for the tasting of each liquid because only new swabs must enter the liquids that are used for tasting.

Procedure: See student lab sheet for instructions.

Answer Key For Questions:
1. Tip/front part of tongue
2. The sides of the tongue
3. The sides of the tongue
4. The tastebuds are located in the front and side edges of the tongue.
5. Answers will vary.
6. Answers will vary. For example, the sense of touch or pain is another unique function.

Literature Links: Aliki. *My Five Senses*. Thomas Y. Crowell, 1989.
Nottridge, R. *Sugars*. Carolrhoda Books, 1992.
Parker, S. *Eating a Meal: How You Eat, Drink, and Digest*. Franklin Watts, 1991.
Wright, L. *Smelling and Tasting*. Raintree Steck Vaughn, 1995.

Portals for Expansion:

Science
- Explore reasons why the common cold can yield a bland taste to all foods. Find out why the sense of smell is helpful when tasting foods.

Mathematics
- Calculate the area of the surface of the tongue that is capable of detecting each taste.

Social Studies
- Research why, over time, some chemicals such as salt and sugar, have been more valuable than at other times in history.
- Invite a chef from a local culinary arts school to discuss how tastes are blended so that prepared foods appeal to all palates.

Language Arts
- Write a letter to a maker of canned vegetables to find out why salt is added to the product.

LAB
Human Body

Map Your Tongue

Procedure:
1. Working with a partner, prepare three paper cups for the taste test.
2. Add 3 mL (one-half teaspoon) of sugar to the first cup. Label the cup "sugar."
3. Add 3 mL (one-half teaspoon) of salt to the second cup. Label the cup "salt."
4. Add enough lemon juice to the third cup so it is about one-eighth full.
5. Pour water into each cup so they are about one-quarter full.
6. Soak one end of a cotton swab in a random cup (sugar, salt, or sour) so that no pattern in established. **Note: Never dip a used cotton swab into a supply cup.**
7. Gently place the cotton swab on the center, sides, and tip of your partner's tongue to find where the taste is sensed.
8. Record where the taste is sensed.

   Test 1, Cup _____:

9. Repeat the test with the remaining cups, using a new cotton swab each time. Record where the taste is sensed.

   Test 2, Cup _____:

   Test 3, Cup _____:

10. Make a drawing of the tongue. Label the regions that sense "sweet," "salty," and "sour."

Questions: *Answer the questions on the back of the paper.*
1. Where does the tongue detect sweet tastes?
2. Where does the tongue detect salty tastes?
3. Where does the tongue detect sour tastes?
4. Where does the tongue have high nerve density?
5. What did you learn about the nerve cells in the tongue?
6. List other nerve cells that have unique functions.

Testing Foods

Purpose:
- Identify, through the testing of various foods, which ones contain carbohydrates, fat, and/or protein.
- Classify foods into groups on the basis of the test results.

Materials Needed:

iodine solution	dissecting needle or long pin
Benedict's solution	paper towel
white photocopy paper	food samples
candle	matches

Introduction: These tests will assist in the classification of a food as carbohydrate, fat and/or protein, but they are not quantitative, they do not reveal how much of that material is in the food sample. Thus, it is likely to obtain mixed results—such as the presence of fat and protein or carbohydrate and protein. It is not the specific answer that is important, but the recognition that foods can be classified through simple testing.

Procedure: See student lab sheet for instructions.

Behind the Scenes: Benedict's solution and iodine solution can be obtained from most high school science departments. However, iodine can also be purchased at low cost from a drug store. Although the food items are not listed, a sample of hamburger, cracker, sugar, apple, butter, potato chips, and cheese are suggested. One interesting approach allows students to bring in additional food samples they wish to test. **Caution:** Neither the chemicals nor the food samples must come close to the mouth. The food, left unrefrigerated, may be bad, and the chemicals are certainly toxic. The flame represents a hazard to loose clothing and long hair. The dissecting needle or pin must be used to stick the food and nothing else.

Literature Links:
Nottridge, R. *Fats*. Carolrhoda, 1992.
Nottridge, R. *Sugars*. Carolrhoda, 1992.
Parker, S. *Eating a Meal: How You Eat, Drink, and Digest*. Franklin Watts, 1991.
Wright, L. *Smelling and Tasting*. Raintree Steck Vaughn, 1995.

Portals for Expansion:
Science
- Compare the results of the testing to the labeling found on the food packaging.

Mathematics
- Rank the foods in order of their carbohydrate, fat, and protein contents by comparing the amounts of each revealed on package labels.
- Compare the package labels of two brands of potato chips to determine which has more protein and which has more fat.

Social Studies
- Invite a dietician to speak to the class regarding the need for a healthful, balanced diet.
- Invite a physician to speak on the variety of diseases that are caused by malnutrition and eating disorders.

Language Arts
- Keep a journal of all food eaten for three days to compare how many carbohydrate foods, fatty foods, and protein foods are eaten.

Testing Foods

Procedure: List the names of the food samples on the chart.

Testing for Carbohydrates—Starches
1. Place a small sample of each food on a paper towel.
2. Add one drop of iodine to a food sample.
3. Watch for a color change.
4. If the iodine turns black, starch is present. Record a "+" on the chart.
5. If it stays reddish brown, no starch is indicated. Record a "–" on the chart.
6. Repeat the steps for the other food samples.
7. Dispose of the food samples.

Testing for Carbohydrates—Sugars
1. Place a small sample of each food on a paper towel.
2. Add one drop of Benedict's solution to a food sample.
3. Watch for a color change.
4. If the Benedict's solution turns a very dark blue-green, sugar is present. Record a "+" on the chart.
5. If the color is light blue-green, no sugar is present. Record a "–" on the chart.
6. Repeat the steps for the other food samples.
7. Dispose of the food samples.

Testing for Fat
1. Place a small sample of each food on a paper towel.
2. Smash a food sample on a sheet of white paper and then remove it.
3. Inspect the mark left behind by the food.
4. If the mark is translucent, fat is present. Record a "+" on the chart.
5. If no mark is left or if the mark is wet but not translucent, no fat is found in the food. Record a "–" on the chart.
6. Repeat the steps for the other food samples.
7. Dispose of the food samples.

Testing for Protein
1. Place a small sample of each food on a paper towel.
2. Place a food sample on the end of a dissecting needle or long pin.
3. Place the sample in the flame of a lighted candle.
4. Put out the flame if the food sample begins to burn.
5. Smell the odor by wafting the smoke to your nose. Gently wave your hand to move the scent towards your face. Do not place the smoking material near your nose.

6. If the odor of sulfur (rotten egg smell) can be detected in the smoke, then the material contains proteins being broken by the heat of the flame. Record a "+" on the chart.
7. Otherwise, record a "–" on the chart.
8. Repeat the steps for the other food samples.
9. When finished, blow out the flame.
10. Dispose of the food samples.

Food Sample	Starch	Sugar	Fat	Protein

+ Nutrient present

– Nutrient not present

Bacteria Hunt

Purpose:
- Predict places where bacteria might live.
- Take a random sample of bacteria from different locations and grow a bacteria culture.
- Draw conclusions about where bacteria may live and its ability to be transmitted to other objects.

Materials Needed:
nutrient rich agar
petri dishes
cotton swabs
distilled water
grease pencil
resealable plastic bags

Introduction: Bacteria can enter the body in a variety of ways and affect many systems and body parts. Examples include bacteria that infect the tonsils resulting in tonsillitis; botulism toxin which is a bacteria that results in food spoilage and food poisoning; and streptococcus which is the bacteria that causes "strep throat." In this activity, students will have the opportunity to predict locations that harbor bacteria, grow the bacteria, and draw conclusions about ways to kill the bacteria.

Setup:
1. Contact the high school biology teacher in your school system and ask him/her to prepare petri dishes with nutrient rich agar for an experiment. These items are usually readily available from a science department.
2. Store the prepared petri dishes with their lids on to prevent airborne bacteria from contaminating them.

Procedure:
1. Engage the class in a discussion about common statements made by parents regarding health and hygiene. Examples to begin the discussion include "Don't put your mouth on the water fountain," and "Always wash your hands after using the bathroom."
2. Once a list of statements has been generated, ask the students for possible explanations as to why these statements are made.
3. Explain to the students that they are going to predict where bacteria may live and breed. Collect their lists of predictions and record them on a chart. Have each group of students choose one of the locations.
4. Follow the instructions on the student lab sheet.
5. Dispose of the petri dishes properly.
6. Conclude the experiment with a discussion about why each of the common statements discussed earlier is important. Also discuss how a person can prevent the spread of bacteria.

Behind the Scenes: Some locations will have plenty of bacteria whereas others which are cleaned every evening will not. You may want to make several extra samples by collecting samples from "not-so-clean" locations such as the wastepaper basket in the bathroom, the water fountain at the end of the day (before it is cleaned), and doorknobs. Safety measures include not allowing the students to handle the bacteria cultures once they begin to grow. The cultures should remain covered to prevent any unnecessary contamination. To prevent contamination, lock each petri dish in a resealable bag. If a student has a cut or scrape on his/her hand, encourage the student to wear rubber gloves while hunting for bacteria. Dispose of the cultures properly by working with your high school science department. It is necessary to kill the growth in a pressure cooker or autoclave (usually available at a high school) or by incineration in a furnace.

Answer Key For Questions:
1. Answers will vary.
2. Answers will vary. For example, wash your hands using soap and water. Clean items on a regular basis with soap or disinfectant cleaning solution.

Literature Links:
Berger, M. *Germs Make Me Sick*. Thomas Y. Crowell, 1985.
Cole, J. *The Magic School Bus Inside the Human Body*. Scholastic, 1989.
May, J., & Stevenson, J. *The Magic School Bus Inside Ralphie*. Scholastic, 1995.
Patent, D. H. *Germs!* Holiday House, 1983.
Richardson, J. *What Happens When You Catch a Cold?* Gareth Stevens, 1984.
Vincent, G. *Feel Better, Ernest!* Greenwillow, 1988.

Portals for Expansion:

Science
• Write to different companies that produce cleaning products requesting information about their products' ability to kill bacteria.
• Analyze commericals for cleaning products. One commercial regarding cleaning products includes a woman stating that another cleaner will only give you "lemon scented germs." Discuss what this means from the perspective of bacteria.
• Research the different types of bacteria that often invade the human body and their effects, such the bacteria on the face that causes acne.

Mathematics
• Draw a grid and illustrate the pattern in which your bacteria grew. Estimate the number of new colonies per day.

Language Arts
• Write a persuasive radio announcement warning people about the need to prevent the spread of bacteria and maintain good hygiene.
• Invite a speaker from the local health agency to speak about communicable diseases.

Art
• Create a poster display that informs members of your school about your findings using pictures and text.
• Develop a series of "health posters" that can be hung throughout your school.

Social Studies
• Research third world countries and their problems with diseases caused by bacteria. Discuss what improvement are needed to eliminate some of the diseases, such as water purification and sewer treatment systems.

Bacteria Hunt

Procedure:
1. Moisten (not soak) a cotton swab in distilled water.
2. Decide where to take a random sample of bacteria by running the cotton swab over the object. For example, if the location is a water fountain, swab the mouthpiece of the fountain.
3. Without touching the swab to any other object, transfer the bacteria sample onto the nutrient rich agar by carefully rolling the cotton swab across the agar. If the agar becomes disturbed the outcome will not be affected.
4. Using a grease pencil, write the name of the location from where the sample was taken on the lid. Include the date.
5. Place the lid on the petri dish and then carefully seal it inside the plastic bag.
6. Check the agar dish every few days and record your observations about what is growing.

Date & Time	Observations	Illustration

Questions: *Answer the questions on the back of the paper.*
1. Where did you collect your bacteria sample?
2. How can you help prevent the spread of bacteria?

Epidemic!

Purpose:
- Participate in a simulated epidemic within the classroom environment.
- Trace the spread of the epidemic to its initiation point.
- Identify ways to help control the spread of infectious disease.

Materials Needed:
For the class
test tubes
eyedroppers or pipettes
0.2M sodium hydroxide
phenolpthalein
water

Introduction: Epidemics have occurred many times over the history of the world. The Black Death plague killed thousands of people in Europe in the 14th century and more recently the Ebola virus surfaced in villages of Africa. Other diseases are said to reach "epidemic" proportions when the number of victims or carriers hit large numbers and the treatments are not working.

Setup:
1. Ask your high school chemistry teacher to make a 0.2 M solution of sodium hydroxide.
2. Prepare a test tube ahead of time that contains the 0.2 M sodium hydroxide solution and set it aside. It is important that you remember which one this is without marking it.
3. Prepare enough test tubes with tap water for the number of students in your class.

Procedure:
1. Give each student a test tube of either the water or the 0.2 M sodium hydroxide solution.
2. It is important to remember which student has the "infected fluids" for later in this activity.
3. Explain to the students that they are going to "share body fluids" by exchanging drops of their solution with other members of the class.
4. Demonstrate how to use a pipette and the proper safety rules which include not squirting other students with the fluids.
5. Have each student exchange two drops with someone else and record it on his/her chart.
6. Continue this process through two or three different cycles, making sure that the exchange happens with a different person each time and is recorded on the chart.
7. Once the exchanges have been completed, ask the students to sit in a circle while carefully holding their test tubes.
8. Walk around the room and place one or two drops of phenolpthalein into each test tube. Some of the solutions will turn different shades of purple if sodium hydroxide is present. Since originally a test tube contained sodium hydroxide and the students mixed fluids by exchanging them, other test tubes will have traces of sodium hydroxide present.
9. Explain to the students that a purple color resulted in a positive test for the cold virus.
10. Challenge the students to trace their patterns back to attempt to find the initial "carrier" of the virus.

Behind the Scenes: This activity can be modified for older students by discussing the AIDS virus or for younger students by discussing how the common cold can be transmitted between people.

Portals for Expansion:
1. Answers will vary. For example, purple or pinkish, or did not change
2. If the solution is purple or pinkish, it was contaminated.
3. Backtrack to study the liquids of others who shared them with you.
4. Fluids can harbor bacteria and viruses which are spread when the fluids are shared.
5. Answers will vary.

Literature Links: Berger, M. *Germs Make Me Sick*. Thomas Y. Crowell, 1985.
May, J., & Stevenson, J. *The Magic School Bus Inside Ralphie*. Scholastic, 1995.
Patent, D. H. *Germs!* Holiday House, 1983.
Vincent, G. *Feel Better, Ernest!* Greenwillow, 1988.

Portals for Expansion:
Mathematics
• Determine what percentage of the class contracted the virus.
Science
• Research how a health organization actually traces a disease back to its origination point.
• Redo this experiment with more exchanges and determine if your chances of contracting a disease are greater.
Language Arts
• Write a short story from the viewpoint of a cold virus about to attack a healthy person. Describe what the virus is thinking and doing.
Health
• Contact the local health department and invite a guest speaker to your classroom to discuss disease prevention and control.

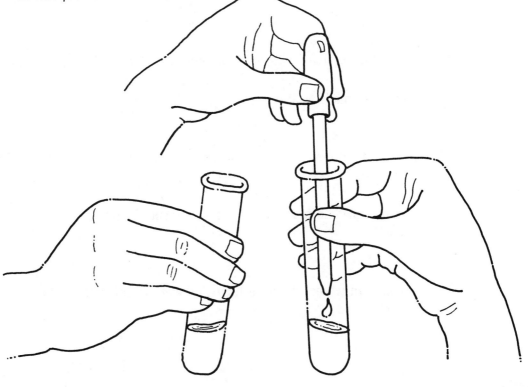

LAB
Human Body

Epidemic!

Procedure: 1. Using the pipette provided by your teacher, place two drops of your liquid into another student's test tube. Have that student add two drops of his/her liquid to your test tube.

2. Repeat Step 1 as many times as directed. Be sure to record each exchange of fluids.

Trial #1: _____ placed _____ drops of fluid into my test tube.

I placed _____ drops of my fluid into _____'s test tube.

Trial #2: _____ placed _____ drops of fluid into my test tube.

I placed _____ drops of my fluid into _____'s test tube.

Trial #3: _____ placed _____ drops of fluid into my test tube.

I placed _____ drops of my fluid into _____'s test tube.

Trial #4: _____ placed _____ drops of fluid into my test tube.

I placed _____ drops of my fluid into _____'s test tube.

Questions: 1. What color did your solution turn when the phenopthalein was added?

2. What does this indicate?

3. How could I figure out who originally was a carrier of the disease?

4. Describe how sharing body fluids can result in transmitting a disease to another person.

5. In your own words, describe how this experiment could simulate the spread of an epidemic.